A
Walk
With
Jesus

Rosalie Willis

Foreword by Ben Torres

Cover by Terrisa J. Olson

A WALK WITH JESUS

Copyright © 1996 by Rosalie Willis

All Rights Reserved

ISBN #0-9650881-0-3

Printed in the United States of America

Second Printing
All Scriptures are taken from the King James
Version of the Bible.

Published by Praise Publishing
708 Dundee
Post Falls, Idaho 83854

Table of Contents

Forward

The art of listening and the ability to correctly discern the voice of God is something that every child of God should desire to become a very vital part of their Christian life. And how blessed we are when we meet someone who has developed these disciplines and is able to share some of the precious truths that God is willing to communicate to every believer who will sit at the feet of Jesus. This is what Rosalie has done in her book, **A Walk With Jesus.** She has shared with us words spoken by God the Father that have ministered to her and will also minister to everyone who reads this book.

I met Rosalie and had the privilege of staying in her home while ministering in Missoula, Montana. During this time it became obvious to me that Rosalie has a deep love for the Lord and has developed a personal relationship with Him through prayer and meditation, which enabled her to write this personal journal.

A Walk With Jesus is not just Rosalie's walk with the Lord, but her book has a prophetic tone which will minister to the reader. While reading the manuscript I felt God speaking encouragement and comfort to my own heart. Therefore, it is with joy that I recommend **A Walk With Jesus** to the body of Christ, and I thank Rosalie for sharing the words the Lord spoke to her heart in her walk with Jesus.

Ben Torres

Ben Torres Ministries
P.O. Box 367
Southington, CT 06489-0367

Preface

April 27, 1989

It was my personal joy to be Rosalie's pastor for several years. When Rosalie asked me to write a few words of introduction for her manuscript, **A Walk With Jesus**, my first thoughts were, "What can I add to this very personal spiritual journey." So my remarks will be directed toward helping you understand her heart, and hopefully as you read this, you will come to know this beautiful lady and her sincere desire to please and serve her Lord.

Rosalie's walk with her Lord and Savior, Jesus Christ, is a result of her study of God's Word. Out of her desire to know God, she has through prayer, meditation and praise sensed the Holy Spirit sharing God's thoughts with her, and in turn has recorded those thoughts into words. Her journey is a very private one, but she desires that we who read this might be able to share in the many ways God has directed her life. I believe you will be blessed and uplifted as you read this personal journal, **A Walk With Jesus**.

Rosalie has made many friends through the years who highly regard her friendship. She is a delightful lady and as you read these words, know that they are coming from a heart filled with love for God, His Word and His church.

It is my prayer that you will be blessed as you read her account of **A Walk With Jesus**.

In Christ's Love,

Rev. Harry L. Ayers

Christian Life Center
Missoula, MT

Introduction

The gift of hearing the voice of God by the power of the Holy Spirit is available to every Spirit-filled born again believer. When I discovered that prayer was a two way street and that God, my Father, longed to share His heart with me, to teach me to trust and obey Him, but especially to know His heart of love, life became an adventure. I began to keep a daily Journal of what God had to say to me, each word a treasure that I never wanted to forget. Lessons of trust and obedience came first, and day-by-day, year-by-year came the exhortation to read, know and have uppermost in my heart, God's Word, the Bible, Scripture, His Parchments. As the days and weeks and years passed by, He taught me of His wonderful, all-encompassing love, building within me a strength and confidence that had never been there before, and an ability to love that had never been there before. His words of wisdom, encouragement, hope, comfort and understanding are available to every Spirit-filled believer who calls Jesus Christ, Savior and Lord.

My prayer is that you, the reader, will also come into this place of communing with God, the Father, through Jesus Christ, your Lord, through the power of the Holy Spirit, to be drawn deeper into His Word, the Scriptures, and to know more deeply His Father's heart of love toward you. He sets the captives free!

Rosalie Willis

Chapter 1

In The Beginning

*"Study to show thyself approved unto God, a workman that
needeth not to be ashamed, rightly dividing the word of truth."*
II Timothy 2:15

Will to know My Word. It is an open door for you that
will never close. My Word is nourishment, it is strength, it
builds faith and is the source through which questions are answered. It is the source of all wisdom and knowledge. Grow
in it. My Word is the instrument through which you shall
grow steadily, and others shall be drawn right along with you.
My Word is the source of life, eternal and abundant. Glory in
it. Know that I am your God. I love you. You need not ever be
afraid. I am always with you, in every thought, word and action. The things of this world will fade away, but My Word
abides forever. Walk fully in it.

Feed on My Word night and day. It is life to you. Lis-
ten closely, My child. I will speak to you as you speak to Me.
Listen well, My child. Much is ahead of you. Stay in My Word.
Prepare yourself.

Be at ease! Be at ease! For I am with you as you are
with Me. My Spirit envelopes you and protects you as do the
flowing robes of the caravan driver protect him from the winds
and sands of the desert. Go forth with praise. Go forth with

thanksgiving. Go forth with the knowledge of My love. I am with you.

Blessed is the one that comes in My Name. Carry the Word as My disciples did. Study well, that you may teach well, that you may carry well My Word. Not only shall My people learn, but you shall learn, also. You shall learn as I put it upon you. Be not impatient, but relax and revel in the luxury of that which you are given. Empires are not created overnight, nor do they last but overnight. My Kingdom will last forever. There is much to know.

Walk with the assurance, my child, that I am with you this day. My love will surround you as you go forth. Praise from your lips shall show others the way. My people shall walk with Me as they see you walk with Me. Enter into My blessings. Walk fully in them. Listen for My voice. You shall know My voice.

Listen, my child. The words you hear are true. You are under My protection when you stay in My Word; live it, and obey it. I promise to protect you through My Word, and My Word is good. Stand firm in your convictions. Look neither to the right nor the left. Stay on the narrow path that leads to life. I am always up ahead, leading. Many are the ways of the world. They are not My ways. They are not to be your ways. Stay in My Word. Once again I say, it is life to you, life everlasting. Praise flows from a full heart. The heart becomes full by reading My Word. Study My Word. Listen for My Word. Keep your spirit open and expect with persistence. Persistence, persistence, all things of My Kingdom come through persistence.

Heed well My Words. Again I say, they are life to you. Praise is the key that unlocks the door to the more abundant life. Your life shall be full, radiant and satisfying as long as you stay in My Word and render praise. Praise Me! Praise Me! Praise Me! Praise Me, and the multitude wandering in the desert shall hear your song of praise and be led to you and thence to whom you serve.

The more you praise, the more you love. The more you love, the more you praise. It's like saying, "Which came first, the chicken or the egg?" They reproduce each other. Love is a total thing, no areas reserved. Praise shall flow from your lips as streams of living water, watering the dry land. Those walking in the desert shall be drawn to Me through your praise, and through the love that praise shall produce. Praise Me! Praise Me!

The spreading of My Word as revealed in My Parchments is a need. You serve Me well when you do this. This is your task, bringing others to know Me, to know the Words of My Parchment and to know how to know Me. This is the prime factor. You shall be led, day-by-day, week-by-week, into that which is your calling from Me. Those who know Me already shall need refurbishing of their faith. This, too, you shall do. You walk in the midst of strangers, yet none are strangers. They shall become of Me through you. Thus it is to be. Amen!

Walk in love. Be guided by it. Stand on My whole Word. Every Scripture is God-breathed. The Word is your arsenal. Meditate on it, chew it and digest it. Standing on My Word is your protection. The Word says, "If Christ sets a man free, he is free, indeed." Stand on that freedom. Reject anything else.

My child, rest in My love. Doubt it not. Stand in it with confidence. Stand straight in that love with confidence. I am within you. You have reason to stand with confidence in Me.

So face the world straight and square and without apology, knowing that I will carry you through in all things. That is standing on My Word.

Depend on Me for every word, every feeling, every action, and then trust that they are from Me. Walk with an assurance and with a carefreeness. Hang loose in Me. Refuse to get uptight. Rebuke fear and doubt every time they show themselves. Fly like a butterfly: relaxed, free, joyful and exuberant. Pour that exuberance out on others, with love. The joy of the Lord is your strength. Appropriate it every morning.

Walk in the Spirit. Hang loose, and let Me work in your life. Do not get uptight and try to reason things out. Seek Me out moment-by-moment. Do not seek your own understanding. Do not go by your own feelings. They are limited. Go, by My Wisdom. It is limitless. The freedom is yours through My Spirit. Trust My Spirit in you. Let it have control. Rise up in your spirit as on eagles' wings. Glide and soar and enjoy the freedom that My Spirit gives and brings. It is yours to enjoy. Rise, fly and enjoy My gift. Don't walk in your own strength. Fly in My strength. Relax and enjoy it.

Place your life in My hands. Fear not. Go forth with a quiet confidence. I am guiding your every thought, word and action. You need not fear. Go forth with the knowledge that I am in command and that My Spirit is within you, guiding you. Continue to prepare. Store up My Word in your heart. Much is ahead.

Follow My Word. Do not stray from it. Soak it up every day. You need nourishment every day. True belief comes from eating My Words. They will sustain you. Thus shall you feed upon Me and draw nourishment from Me.

Be still, and know that I am God. The child that trusts and obeys his parents enjoys many more privileges. So it is in the Kingdom of God. The child who digests My Word and obeys it walks in much more from Me than the child who lets things come and go as they may. I am the rewarder of them who diligently seek Me. Much is coming. You must prepare. Continue digesting My Word.

Rise up early. It is in the early morning hours that your spirit can soar. It is like a launching pad from which it can take off and soar through the day. Meaningless avenues can be short-circuited in this way. You start in My will and stay in My will for the rest of the day. Listen with intentness to the heart-cry of those around you and lift them up in intercession. Intercede as I will lead you. Praise Me in their names. Let the Words of My mouth and the meditation of your heart by alike one to the other. I will direct your path, every thought, word and action. Step out in faith, believing. Do not hold back. I am with you. I will not let you stumble. Walk in My peace.

Enter into My rest. It is a place reserved for you. Praise is a vehicle toward that rest. Put that vehicle into high gear and don't let off the throttle. Praise is the vehicle into My perfect joy. Burst forth into its fullness. Praise is the vehicle into My perfect love, in which there can be no fear. Perfect love casts out all fear and praise is the vehicle to perfect love. Stay in that vehicle at all times. It is a protection to you.

Stay in My Word. It imparts faith. The Word of God will not benefit you unless its hearing is mixed with faith, and faith leads to action. This, then, is eating My Word. Real food mixes with the juices in your stomach [faith] and is turned into energy [actions].

Prayer is much like My Word. It must be consumed with faith and comes out belief. Presumption comes in when one bypasses a one to one relationship with Me. That person knows of Me, knows about Me, knows that I am and that I am a gracious God, but has not consulted with Me to find out My will, but presumes to know My will from others' previous experiences. I cannot be put in a box. My ways are higher than your ways. Again I say, "Does My Word not say, if one desires wisdom, just ask and I shall supply it?" First know My perfect will in a situation through My Word and communion with Me. Then stand on that word in faith and believe. So be it.

The spirit of anxiety, the spirit of anticipation, often causes physical man to be out of balance. Patience is the key, one of the keys to My Kingdom. Be not impatient, lest the key turn on an empty lock. Worshiping Me in My House and getting to know Me, My life and My Parchments shall not only relieve the spirit of anxiety and desire, but is the way to My Way.

Those who stand with Me often suffer the slings and arrows of outrageous fortune; yet they are blessed, they shall be blessed, they are blessed, and My blessing shall overcome all inequities. As long as you walk in and with My Spirit, you shall be righteous. No one shall take from you that which I have given you, that which I have shared with you. Stick with it, for the Words of My Spirit are meaningful and lasting. Mind not, mind not the slings and arrows of outrageous fortune, for they shall not harm you. Keep your faith, and I shall refresh you, strengthen you and lead you. Tarry not over wonderings as to that which you are to do for Me, for I shall show you, be with you and guide you when least you expect. That which is to be shall be, and you shall know what is to be in My time. My child, take heart; do not be distressed. I am with you and direct all your paths. Nothing can harm you. My ways are higher than your ways. It is not always necessary to understand. Just run with Me. I will clear the path. You need not be afraid. Stay in My Word. Feed on it. It will keep you free.

Continue step-by-step, each following the other without haste. All shall come to pass as I have said. Fret not, worry not, simply praise and rejoice. Listen, My child, and hear My voice. My children need never go astray. My Presence is always with them. I am there always to lead them in the right direction, if they will only ask and listen.

I am the Lord your God. I shall defend you. Let not the spirit of fear come into you. Resist it. Self-will, that will I give to you, put it into practice. Many are the opportunities to sit back and let the tide overcome you. I have given you the will to overcome. Use it. The tides of the storm are always waiting, more than willing to overcome, but a child of the King has the power to be an overcomer. Be aware at all times. Satan comes as a roaring lion ready to devour. Wear My armor at all times, and be prepared. Do not let piety stick its head in the window and rob you of your strength and purpose.

Piety is a spirit that comes in through rejection, the desire to be accepted by trying to be good enough, to try to deserve to be accepted. A child of God does not have to try to be good enough. He is counted as worthy because of My Son's death on the cross. This is your covering, your righteousness. You could never make yourself good enough by your strivings. The spirit of piety seeks to gauge a person's worth through the eyes of other people. True piety from God, not Satan's counterfeit, seeks to please God, is not motivated by approval from man. Look to the Lord for your approval. Keep your eyes off man. Stand straight as an arrow looking neither to the right nor left, but straight up.

Stand tall and straight, knowing I am your deliverer. Aggressive appropriation is the key. Reject fear daily. Reject piety daily. Praise Me daily. Keep your swept house filled with Me. Move ever onward. Blessed is the one who walks with Me moment-by-moment. Nothing can come nigh him. Nothing can hinder his walk, because his eyes are set on Me. He is positioned in Me. He cannot be moved. Perseverance; not passivity. Rebuke the passivity that tries to stick its nose in the window. It has no power over you, as long as you stand in My power and rebuke it.

Stick with it, My child. Narrow is the way, but by strict adherence to My Word and persistence in listening to My voice, the path is passable. My hand is over you, My child, like an umbrella. Stray not from underneath it through doubt and unbelief. My righteousness will prevail in your life, as long as you do not doubt. It is when you doubt that you try to grab hold of your own righteousness again, through insecurity and fear. He who believes at all times does not experience insecurity and fear, for they are not of Me.

Chapter 2

Victory Through The Word

"All Scripture is given by inspiration of God,
and is profitable for doctrine, for reproof, for correction,
for instruction in righteousness:"
II Timothy 3:16

By giving you the vision of how I see you through My Word, line by line, precept by precept, you are becoming as I see you. Stick with it. The joy is in becoming that person by becoming more and more in My image. It will be real joy and in no way counterfeit. Patience.

My child, walk this day with faith, knowing your sins are forgiven. Burst forth into the sunshine. Bask this day in the warmth of My love. My love shall be your love. Appropriate it, walk in it, it is yours. Springs of living water shall pour forth from you. Don't doubt. It is and shall be.

The days ahead will be filled with confusion. You will have to know where you stand. You will have to know My way of thinking, to know what is happening and why. Lay the groundwork well, for the time is short. You will need the strength of My Word within you. Press in. Face each new day with the strength of My Word. It will carry you through the day unscathed.

Many things will come to pass that are not understandable to human comprehension. Carry on with the knowledge that My will was carried out. My ways are not always peaceful. They had much to learn. You had much to learn. Set your mind at rest and go on your way.

Keep your family lifted up to Me in all prayer and supplication, claiming the Power of the Blood over them. Persecution shall come, but stand straight and tall, for I have overcome the world. Walk in My strength. It shall be sufficient. Abound in joy, My joy. You shall know My joy and peace in the battle. Stand your ground.

Continue this day free in the way you speak. There is no fear. I am with you, guiding and directing you. Relax in that knowledge. Put into practice that freedom in the spirit which you possess. It is yours. Do not shrink back from habit. You are an overcomer. Stand straight and tall. You are a child of the King. It is a day of victory. Rejoice! Rejoice!

It is a day of liberty and freedom, a day of victory and defeat, the defeat of Satan and a renewed and enlarged knowledge of that defeat. You are to walk in this knowledge. You are to put this knowledge into practice and set the prisoners free. Many they will be and many their needs, but the victory is assured. Enter into the warfare with vigor. Minister with praise and thanksgiving, for the victory is yours.

Today is another day of victory and rejoicing. Proceed with strength of spirit and joy. I am bringing My pure love and joy into your life. Press on. Every day they become more a part of you.

Know that as long as you walk in My power, in My Spirit, you do not need to fear the evil one. You shall know what is of Me. Press onward. Never retreat. Press into the meat of My Word. Saturate yourself with My Word, so you can speak, teach and impart My Word.

Pile up My Words in your heart. Make of your heart a storehouse. My Words will guide and comfort you. I am with you, to guide you, moment-by-moment. Praise Me, and rejoice. Rejoice evermore. Everything through a praising heart comes out joy and gladness. Rejoice in everything. Praise Me in all things. I will lead you, My child, gently and with care. Do not ever fret. Patience! It has to be wrought in the spirit, step-by-step. Worry not with the minute, but keep your eye on the big picture. What is past, is past. The need is for that which is to come.

Shake off your doubt like a second skin. Ask of Me, listen, and believe. Your desires become My desires, because I put them within you. Follow your leadings. They come from Me. When you walk in the Spirit, you will not have desires of the flesh. My Spirit directs your desires. So do not doubt. My child, My child, praise Me, rejoice in Me day-by-day, and delight in Me, for I delight in you. Walk with a light heart. My joy is your joy.

Stick with it, My child. The blessings are yours to be walked in, now and forever. You have done well. The victory is yours, day-by-day. Stand in that victory, and claim new ground. Be not impatient. Keep moving, and My armor shall protect you. No need to fear. Fear is never from Me. Condemnation is never from Me. My Words you shall hear. Fear not. Ask for wisdom. It shall be yours. Depend on the Holy Spirit to bring to remembrance all you shall need. It shall be. Come expecting and rejoicing.

My teaching is perpetual and leads to immortality and everlasting life in the Spirit. Through the Spirit and your faith and boldness, you shall know eternal life, happiness and peace. You have the brass ring of the merry-go-round of life. Through this leading, you shall see others grab the brass ring of life, and yea, though you walk through the valley of the shadow, there is no need to fear evil, for I am with you, and together we shall climb to the peak, wherein lies the Kingdom.

Rest in My love. Don't allow yourself to get uptight. Take it day-by-day. Allow Me to fill your days. Every morning, turn the day over to Me. Ask for My leading, and it shall be yours. Don't doubt your leadings. They come from Me. Waste not a minute in fear, doubt or unbelief. They cause the bondages. Don't stop on your way rejoicing to look at the devastation around you. Keep your eyes upward. Spread joy and belief. It is contagious. I am with you.

You need not have the feeling of frustration, void, nor empty feelings, when the crutch of books and tapes are not there, as long as My Parchment is there. The books and tapes supplement My Word, and were they to be missing, you would find strength in My written words, My Parchment, in My laws. The strength of My Word from the scrolls of My Parchments shall be the rock and the shield. All else merely amplifies the original. Take strength, sustenance, glory and dominion in the reading of My Word. The glories of the heavens open to the readers, doers and those who walk in My Word.

Lift up your heart in praise this day. Let Me carry your grievances. You walk with a light heart. Don't judge others' actions. Let Me do the judging. Go on your way, rejoicing. Don't allow dark clouds to hover near. Use the authority I gave you to loose yourself from them. Praise closes the door to bondages. They can't latch hold of a praising heart. That is why you must praise Me in all circumstances and at all times. It is a protection to you.

The tools of the Spirit are inside you, and the tools are Me. You go with Me and be the channel through which I may perform the miracles, the channel through which My power flows. Keep your spirit open to Me. It is not what you do. It is what you will allow Me to do through you. The clothes of the Spirit are first accepted, walked in and believed, and then they become a reality, seen of all people.

Be not afraid of your convictions. They are from Me, too. Stand up for what you feel is right at the time. The child who walks with Me knows his feelings, leadings and convictions are from Me. Stand up, stand up for Jesus. Standing up for your convictions is standing up for Me. Denying your convictions is denying Me. Straightforwardness is a virtue. My Son was straightforward, and you are to be as My Son. Honesty is always the best policy. It places all on sure footing. Play it straightforward, and let Me worry about the results.

Have you not been given to act and perform as My channel? You have been pointed in the direction and given the oats to spread. So kick up your heels and burst forth, as a runner in a grueling race, for, yea, you are a runner in My Name. You are running to pass the news of My Word to a hungry nation. I shall lead you in the teaching of the Holy Spirit, My Spirit, for you will stand strong and stick to your guns. Cast out doubt. Cast out fear and apprehension, for they have no part in the doing of My Word, nor in the speaking out of My Word and about My Word. My Word shall ring forth with the clarion sound of a bell from your lips.

My songbird shall sing out with glorious praise to Me. The words of praise to Me shall sink into the marrow, muscle and hearts of those who hear. By these songs of praise shall the oppression of the listeners be lifted. They shall think My power and My glory is what it takes to lift them from the sinews and depths of their everyday doldrums. Thus shall My Word be spread. Sing out with boldness and strength, which shall show in the softness, the beauty and the truth of My Word.

Love is forgetting one's self and recognizing the other fellow. Straightforwardness too is a form of love. The opposite is withdrawal and concentration on one's self and one's needs. Straightforwardness concentrates on others and worries not about how they will react and feel about you because of your honesty and love for them. I love you, and you are worthy of love. Further looking to one's own need for love is not necessary nor profitable. Seek first the Kingdom, and all these things will be added unto you. The Heavens open wide to the person who concentrates on the other fellow's needs. You cross the bridge to that person, and I will bridge the gap between surface concern and true deep concern. I will pour My love through you into the situation.

My guidance is yours for the asking. I delight in guiding My children. Simply walk step-by-step in expectation. To the one who has much, much will be given. The more revelation and awareness you walk in, the more you will receive. It is a never ending spiral upward of joy. The one who walks in expectation receives much. Therefore, walk, expecting My guiding hand upon your life moment-by-moment, for it is yours. Those that expect little receive little. Ask much, and you will receive much.

Fear not, My child. I shall guide you step-by-step, and you shall not stumble nor cause others to stumble. Do not become impatient with yourself or with Me. All is moving according to My timing. Cast out impatience. My plans shall not be thwarted. Much more is being accomplished than you are aware of. Simply move as I direct and claim the ground in My Name.

Hear My Voice

"My sheep hear My voice and I know them and they follow Me."
John 10:27

My children that are called by My Name shall hear My voice. It is their inheritance. But if they do not know that it is their inheritance, how shall they receive it, and if they do not accept that inheritance, how shall they receive it? Continue spreading the Good News. Continue planting the seed. When results are not forthcoming, worry not. Leave it in My hands. You simply be obedient to your calling. Plant the seeds I give you to plant. Water the ones I give you to water, and harvest the ones I give you to harvest. Do not move outside My will through human motives. Follow My leading.

`Fill your days with My Presence. Praise fills the void when understanding is lacking. You will know in due time that which is My will, that which is to be of Me. Cast out fretting.

You are doing better in your walk with Me. Be not disheartened; be not discouraged, but keep your faith in Me, for I shall lift you up. I have lifted you up, and I shall continue to lift you up.

Much has been prepared for you. You are coming more and more into the revelation of it. Perseverance is bringing it about. My radiance shall shine on you like the dawn of a new day, or as the sun beaming through the clouds. My people shall see My radiance through you, the radiance of My love, the radiance of My smile upon them. Continue to stand fast, and you shall walk step-by-step into all that I have prepared for you. Continue on with heightened anticipation and joy for all I have reserved for you. Delight yourself in the Lord, and He will give you the desires of your heart. This is a true saying, and so it will be and is with you.

My people shall hear My voice. More and more they shall walk in My way. My way shall shine forth as a beacon light upon My people, and those tottering on the borderline shall find themselves drawn to that light. Continue to shine forth as that beacon light. The words that you speak are not as important as the love and light of My smile that pours through you to them. Feed on Me and My Word, and keep your vessel full to overflowing. The overflow will catch them like honey.

Your focus on Me is vital, My child. When your focus is sharp, all else falls into line. Listen quietly, My child. Still your inner being. I can overcome the outside disturbances, so you can hear My voice above the din, but it is in the stillness that real fellowship with Me is found. Communion with Me is a two-way street. It must be pursued with diligence and regularity. Don't let the trials of this world intervene. My light shall shine out through all the dark corners. New areas of your life shall come to light that have not been revealed before. Communion with Me does not come through self-preservation or a desire for self-preservation. It comes through a step-by-step resignation of self. Each section of self you turn over to Me, I replace with fullness, My fullness and overflow.

Communion is based on overflow. Overflow brings desire and openness for communion. Listen attentively, My child.

My thoughts are not your thoughts. My ways are not your ways, but I put My thoughts within you and a desire for My ways. Fear not that you will not know My ways and desires for you, for they come about naturally to the seeking, open heart. Ponder My Words in your heart. This is how they become a part of you. This keeps your mind set on Me, and not on the passing scene. A mind set on Me will never be disappointed. The mind set on Me is open to conversation with Me and continual communion with Me. The mind set on Me is closed to contamination. The mind that is set on Me is like the rudder of a ship. It keeps the ship always headed in the right direction. The mind set on Me can run on automatic pilot, with no fear of doubt, with Christ at the helm. Christ is the creator and navigator of your ship. Rest in His complete control, in whatever course He wants to take.

Carry forth My Word with ease. Do not get tense or uptight. Relax. Let Me perform My will through you. You are the ax blade. I swing the handle. The closer you nestle in, the more confident you can be of walking in My perfect will. That is why I say, "Keep your mind fixed on Me." There is peace and safety within the safety of My wing.

That which you experienced was of My doing, that you might know and experience the confusion which others, not walking with me, endure. Thus, you who walk with Me have been made aware of, and will be better equipped to minister to, and help those who do have confusion. You can now recognize it, and be able to more quickly and smoothly walk in a helpful manner. You no longer have confusion, for you have bound it and cast it out.

Surely My Grace shall be sufficient for you. I shall sustain you. I shall test you, but I shall never let you go. My Glory shines about you as a protection. Nothing can penetrate the protection of My light. Nothing happens without My permission to those who walk closely with Me. Incline your ear and listen more attentively. Do not allow the pressure of the moment to topple you. Rely on Me in all instances. I knew of, and know of, each detailed happening, and of its outcome. Don't sweat it. Rejoice and sing a new song of praise unto your Lord, who is your fortress and your shield.

My ways are constantly being made known to My children. Those that have ears to hear, shall hear. Dedication to My Word, lack of legalism, and praise and worship open the ears, that they might hear. Appropriation, day-by-day is the key, a continual focus on Me. Forthrightness of spirit opens the door to purity of spirit. Forthrightness allows the impurities to rise to the surface to be dealt with, instead of hiding them deep within. Impatience breeds doubt, and mistrust. Bind and cast out impatience when it raises its head.

Did I not say, "I am in control?" Did I not say, "Rest from your worry and anxiety and trust in Me?" Continue on in perfect trust in My guidance over you and those you love, for I love them too, and they are under My protection. Cease from your worrying over the sibling. Let Me continue to lead you and guide you by the Spirit. All will turn out right, as I would have it. Turn the whole burden of her upbringing over to Me. I, her Creator, know better how to mold her. Keep her laid upon the altar of your spirit, that I might continue to be the one to mold her spirit.

My ways are full of life and joy to the one who follows after them. It is the beginning of eternal life, gladness, joy and peace. My people shall glory daily in the freedom that joy brings. Freedom in the spirit brings My pure joy and freedom from bondages.

Cast out doubt, fear and apprehension, for they have no part in the doing of My Word, nor in the speaking out of My Word to a hungry nation. The dross is being burned out. A more perfect thing is coming forth in your life. Purity of spirit, soul and body is the goal. I see you as pure, but it is being wrought within you, step-by-step. The joy is in the becoming. Hesitate not.

You have learned mighty and glorious truths. Ponder them in your heart. Delight in them. Digest them further. My sheep shall hear My voice. They shall hear and rejoice. They shall no longer walk in darkness. They shall see the light and make their way toward that light. Glory, in the Highest! My people shall have ears to hear and eyes to see, and they shall go forth as a mighty army of the Lord. Break forth in singing, for the time has come to rejoice mightily, for the Glory of the Lord shall shine upon His people, and they shall not doubt nor fear, but they shall move out with confidence, knowing their Lord is going before them, making straight the path. Glory, Hallelujah!

Chapter 4

Enter Into My Rest

"And He said,
My presence shall go with thee, and I will give thee rest."
Exodus 33:14

My Spirit descends as a dove and rests gently and lightly upon those who profess My Name. It rests as joy immeasurable. It rests as a protective shield. Be a confident runner in My race, knowing My umbrella of protection follows over you, just as the cloud went ahead of the Israelites by day and the fire by night. As long as you are running in My race, you will not run out from under My protection. Confidence in Me is the key. Confidence that I will never let you down. Run with courage, persistence, singleness of mind and a continual focus on Me.

My child, you do not have to defend Me. It is I who defend you. You spoke My Word, the Word I gave you. My Word does not fall to the earth void. I send it out to accomplish the task for which I sent it. Don't try to explain it, don't try to reason it, for have you not read in My Scripture that My thoughts are not your thoughts? Fret not! Worry Not! It is I who spoke the words. It is I who shall fulfill the words. It is only for you to stand, believing in My Word. I shall give you far more than you have thought to ask for. It is all right to appear foolish, for is it not in My Parchment that I will use the foolish to confound the wise? Appear foolish, and rejoice in your wisdom, which shall come from Me.

Put down your guard and walk in the fullness of the Spirit. Don't try to explain things, simply state the facts; spread My Word. My Word does not need embellishment. It stands on its own. Speak it without apology. Simply speak it. Break forth. You are loosed. Break forth from your cocoon and soar.

Break forth into new life. My people shall break forth as the new dawn. Loose yourself from the self-imposed re-strictions of actions, reactions and attitudes. Have your ears al-ways open toward Me to receive My leadings. Don't move in the old ways just because they have worked in the past. They won't work in the future. The old wine worked and sufficed, too, but if one held onto it, one would never know the joys of the new. It is a new day. Walk fully in it.

My Glory shall shine about you as the noonday sun. You are being established and well grounded. Your way has been made straight. You shall be the Pied Piper along that straight and narrow path. Walk jubilantly!

In proportion to your liberality of praise expressed will be My generosity in infinite magnitude. Labor not to analyze each need. Leave diagnosis and mechanics in My hand. Com-plexities exist only in your mind from the enemy to dull your faith. Ignore them. You be, and I will do!

Remove the spirits of impatience, uncertainty and doubt, for I have led you in the past and will continue. Forever be on your guard against frenzied activity. My way is with a quiet assurance, confidently walking one step at a time. Stead-fastly and firmly My Son walked this earth with love and com-passion; so are you to walk.

You placed the problem, which was no problem, with Me, for there is only one way, My Way. The clouds of apprehension, anxiety and panic have been brushed aside, and the heavens are cloudless again. As you ask, so shall you receive. Ask with the heart. Ask from the heart and not from the mind.

Strengthen your desire to love through the reading of My Word. Reading and pondering My Word on love will produce that openness through which I can channel My love. Pursue love. The gift is yours through perseverance and awareness. Press on.

Was not My Word in the beginning? Has not My Word been? My Word is, for all is in My Word. As you stand on My Word, so shall I stand with you. The carnal mind does not come from Me. My Word comes through the spirit, and you who believe in Me and My Word shall know the full glory, the full meaning of My Kingdom. Stand up; stand on My Word. Be My Word! They who know not My Word shall know My Word, for you shall proclaim it in thought, word and deed through the leading of My Spirit. You are lifted up. My strength is your strength. Fear not for words to speak, for I shall give them to you, and they shall be of strength. There are no strangers in My Kingdom, for they who speak My Word and live My Word, are My Word.

Meditate on My Word night and day. A deeper understanding of My Word comes as you grow spiritually, but you must continually be in My Word to receive the gift, that continual gift of fuller understanding. Do not limit Me through your neglect of My Word.

Again I say, "Doubt not, fear not, do not back off, but stand fast." Stand firm and know I am with you, and you walk surrounded by and with My power, My love and My strength. The heavenlies know not time as does the mind of man. Man has a need to slow down from the rushing and thrashing about on the earth, and in so doing man shall be able to grasp and understand the fullness, the richness and the glory of that which is My Heavenly Kingdom. The changes and happenings are continuous, each fitting in its place as a part of a puzzle. Feel proud in My Word. Stand up for My Word. Be not a doubter. Be not of little faith, but shout, "Hallelujah!" and stand firm.

Stand strong. Stand strong in the joy of My Presence. You walk down a narrow path, but one flooded with light, the light of My Presence and understanding. I shall not let you down. You shall not stumble. The oil of gladness shall be upon your head. Bubble over. Others need that oil of gladness bubbling over upon them.

My light shines through the darkness and makes that darkness light, pure light that cannot be extinguished. The light of the Word shines through a person and lights up the innermost being like an x-ray, exposing the hidden problems, that they might come to light and be healed. Come to that light. Bask in the warmth of that light. The warmth and love of that light bring healing to the spirit, soul and body.

By faith man walks with Me. The carnal mind seeks to box Me in, to figure out each detail. The carnal mind seeks to anticipate all My moves and to crow about them. The humble inherit My Kingdom. Far better be it to walk with a constant awareness of My Presence and My guidance than to seek Me as one would a horoscope or a fortune teller. With faith one walks with assurance, without fear or apprehension. So are you to walk.

Worship Me in spirit and in truth, for through worship is real fellowship with Me found. Worship opens up the human spirit to Me. Worship takes down the walls that would keep Me out. True worship brings right standing with Me, for it breaks down all the barriers and opens the door for communion and fellowship on a one-to-one basis. Raise up your voice in singing to Me, and I shall hear and rejoice in thee. Raise up your voice in praise and thanksgiving. Make a joyful noise and rejoice.

Fear not! Fear not! For I know the state of mind and that which is in the heart and know how best to show My love. Simply trust Me, and obey that which I give you to do. I will do the rest. Bring forth with assurance that which I give you. Steady yourself, and stand firm as a rock. Brace yourself on the Word. Blessed is he who walks with the assurance in his heart that I will never fail him. Blessed is he who steps out with faith, believing. Be blessed of the Lord. Do not be swayed by fear nor doubt nor an unbelieving heart. Abundance and joy come to the heart that is focused on Me and it cannot be moved. Be steadfast and immovable in your stand of faith in Me.

One who walks with Me, and one who knows Me, is protected from the enemy by the cloak of My Spirit. A warning of that which is not of Me suffices to set the alarm bells ringing. That teaching that is not mine shall not ring true in the light of that which is My Scripture, and that which is not of Me shall set off the alarms. Claim the protection, and it shall be.

Do not worry and ponder over the mechanics of My dealings in your life. Simply follow My leadings. My dealings in your life and in the lives of those around you bring about that steadfastness and sureness of foot in your walking with Me that you long for. Step-by-step it is coming forth in you and in the lives of those you love. The Kingdom comes without observation, but it comes. It is coming forth step-by-step in you and in those whom you lift up to Me. Trust and obey, for there is no other way. It is the way to complete fulfillment. Walk in it.

Haste not, be not impatient, for My leadings fall one upon the other in an orderly fashion. All shall come to pass as I would have it for those who love Me and follow My commands and leadings. I shall not desert you nor forsake you nor your household. Pressure is applied by the evil one. My ways bring peace no matter what the surrounding circumstances may be. Peace be with you.

Break forth in singing this day. Fill the air with your joy. Fill your home with My Glory by speaking out My Words with joy, gladness, power and truth. Pour forth that which is in your heart and has been welled up. Pour it forth and I will fill it up again.

Labor not to fulfill My will. Enter into My rest. Believe, and praise My Name. He whose focus is continually set on Me shall continually know My will, and I shall fulfill My will through him, and he shall delight in Me and I in him. Praise and thanksgiving are not only a continual protection to My children, but they are the vehicle through which I abide in them and they abide in Me. I inhabit the praises of My people. Rejoice this day, for the desires of your heart are the desires of My heart, and they are and shall be. Hallelujah! Sing praises! For great days are ahead for those who continue to march forth at My direction. Much is ahead for the singing, joyful, praising, thankful heart. Bask in the sunshine of My smile, and others will be touched and blessed from the extending rays.

Relax and fret not, for My Word shall come through. Continue to wait upon My Word with regularity. Do not let our relationship take second place in your priorities. Come to Me with expectancy, and I will respond. My little lambs run and jump and play gleefully, but they are always aware of My Presence. They know I am their Shepherd, and they obey instantly when I call. They become My sheep and recognize My voice clearly. Practice My Presence continually. Relax and enjoy My Presence.

As you walk with Me, many new things will unfold to you. You are headed on a high adventure. Rejoice along the way. Sing praises as you go, and stay close behind Me as I lead. All is going according to schedule. Relax and enjoy each day as it comes. Look for My hand in each happening. Learn to recognize My hand consistently. Enter in with all your heart. Do not fear the giants. They are only illusions. The only reality is what I say is reality and I say, "Enter in." All is prepared for you. Partake, enjoy and appropriate.

Chapter 5

Be My Word

*"Let the Word of Christ dwell in you richly in all wisdom;
teaching and admonishing one another in psalms and hymns
and spiritual songs, singing with grace in your hearts to the Lord."*
Colossians 3:16

My Word is Spirit, and it is life. Those that hear My Word, though they be dulled of hearing, shall have My Word work within their spirit. Continue to speak My Words for they bring life to those whom they touch. Receive My Word and extend it to others. Take in and give out continually. Be My Word, speak My Word, be a manifestation of it to others. Continue to listen for My Word and to encourage others to diligently listen, for from this dedication come blessings beyond measure. It is the open door to a walk with Me. Continue! Continue! Let not up nor be distracted. Herein lies the key to all things in My Kingdom. They are all yours. This is the channel through which you take possession of what I have already proclaimed to be yours. Do not hold back. Enter in with all your heart. Do not doubt nor waver. Enter in with abandonment and trust. Come with expectation and I shall respond.

The word for today is, "Relax." Do not let not down your guard against the spirit of anxiety. My will shall come forth through you. Be pliable, not uptight. Let My Spirit flow. Do not bind it through anxiety and tension. The time is there.

My time is there. Trust Me! Trust Me! Do you not trust Me?
Yes, you do. Now show it. Relax!

The dedication of My children is joyous to Me. It is
through this dedication that I, the perfecter of their faith, can
polish and shape My precious stones. Dedication brings about
quality and perfection. Give Me your dedication so that I
might give you My perfection. The level of your dedication
dictates the level of perfection, the level of exchange. So aspire
to a high level. This brings mutual joy and fellowship. Do not
be satisfied with little. Reach for and aspire to all that I have in
store for you. The more you give to Me of the total dedication
of yourself, the more I pour into you My attributes, My perfection.

My Words to you shall rise up from your heart. They
shall be a gushing forth and not a trickle. You shall be My
mouthpiece, to speak My Words. Pour forth My Words without hesitation. Come often to the well, that it might overflow
through you. Your words shall be My Words, for I shall put
them within you. Press forth, renewed in that knowledge. Rivers of living water shall flow, and you shall know My will.
Speak My Words. Speak them forth. Does one practice giving
forth of My Spirit? No! Give forth. That which comes forth
shall be from the heart. Practice for this compounds the errors.
Speak My Words with the understanding of your heart and not
the understanding of your mind, for the mind is an enmity
against Me. Speak My Words forth boldly. Take My Word to a
hungry people that know Me not but hunger to know My
peace. I shall shower My blessings upon them through you.
Do not let them down. Open your heart to those around you.
Open your heart to discern their needs, for the needs of My
people are many. Be that helping, open channel through which
I can pour My love and compassion. Let not apathy nor passivity rise up to hinder My Spirit from reaching out to them, to

heal My people in mind, body and spirit. Let Me minister to My people's needs through you. Those through whom I can minister healing and deliverance are few. They must be dedicated to speak My Word, to be My Word, to minister My Word to a hungry people.

Rise forth and carry well My message of healing and salvation to My hungry people. Many they shall be that shall come to you, and you shall speak My Words of comfort to them, for they know not My ways, but you shall teach them My ways. You shall teach them My ways with spirit and with truth. Till the soil that I shall give you. Till it fervently and with joy. Let the joy of your countenance shine forth. Continue to let others bask in it. Stretch forth your hand in blessing to many that I shall give you to bless. Be My lightning rod of blessing to many. Bask in My light upon you. It shall shine. It shall shine. Be not concerned over others' reactions. Simply bask in that light, and rest in the warmth of My love.

It has been a time of learning, and now you are as a swimmer tossed into the pond. You shall swim, you shall discern, and you shall know. For have you not had the battleground, the 40 months in the wilderness, and have I not led you through the wilderness to know that which is My will and to know that which is from Me and is by Me? And the teaching shall come forth. And in your new oasis you shall not be alone. More shall know of Me, of My power, of My Glory, of My Kingdom. Go forth with a bright spirit within your heart, for it shall be My bright Spirit. Hallelujah, for now another shall go forth as it says in My Parchment to preach My Gospel and spread My Word. Praise and peace be among and to My people. Again I say, peace unto My people, for they shall know peace and joy and understanding.

You have grasped that which is from Me, My Word. My Word comes to you both from without and from within. More than signs and wonders shall come forth, and more of Me shall be made real through the inner approach which you give forth to others. Go forth, for blessed is he who comes in My Name. The word which you are to carry is not "I come," but it is, "I AM NOW!"

My people shall be My praise upon the earth. Bring forth that abundant praise to Me, that you too may become My praise upon the earth. My praisers are a mighty force, greater than any other force upon the earth, to bring down strongholds and to open up the way for righteousness to prevail. And prevail it shall! It is the choice of each individual to be a part of or not be a part of this end time army of praisers, My praisers. Open up your heart to Me and let Me fill it with My radiance and praise. Praise, and prevail.

My house, the house of My Word, shall rise forth as a mighty army, carrying My banner and proclaiming My Word. Each member is like a tiny spark that will ignite small portions in many different areas that shall explode and cause a mighty bonfire that will consume the whole area and bring My people together in unity, love and a mutual hungering after My Word and My ways. Rejoice, for My Word shall ring forth as a clarion call of a bell, bringing My people in out of the wilderness, into the protection and warmth of the shadow of My wing.

Glorious are the days ahead, and glorious shall be the acts of My hand. Many shall see and know that I am the Lord God, maker of all things, and they shall rejoice and give thanks. Rejoice, rejoice, for the days are upon us of great magnitude, and My people shall come to Me and know My voice and love My ways. Rejoice! Rejoice! Rejoice!

Chapter 6

Ready In Due Season

*"The Lord God hath given me the tongue of the learned,
that I should know how to speak a word in season to him that is weary. "*
Isaiah 50:4a

Fear not, for the time is mine. There shall be sufficient time. Break forth into singing, for the day shall be bright, the day shall be full and productive, the day shall be Mine. Listen well, My child, as you go through the day. My leadings will come as you move step-by-step. You can worship as you work. As you walk, keep your mind focused on Me. My peace is with you. When more is needed, stretch forth your hand and draw more. It is always there. Draw upon it. Burst forth with radiance this day. Don't smother My bright spirit within. Let it out. Set it free through fluent praises.

Relax, and enjoy that which comes your way day-by-day. Each day, that which I have for you will surely come your way. So, fret not as to what you shall do and where you shall go. You shall know. You shall know. Rejoice at the opening of doors, and rejoice at the closing of doors. Both are by My hand. Strain not. Relax, and let Me fill your days to overflowing.

Move forthrightly! Move straightforwardly! Move without fear or reservation. Move lovingly, knowing that it is My Spirit within you, and knowing that if you speak My

Words, I will perform the miracles and wonders through those words. Do not back off. Let those who come in contact with you know where you stand and who directs your life, and through whom comes your peace, joy, understanding, strength and bright spirit. Do not cheat them of this understanding.

Resist the enemy, and he shall flee from you. Magnify My Word. Expand it in your experience and in your understanding, through constant use. Allow it the chance to constantly germinate and take root in your life through intake, through the power of the Holy Spirit, My Holy Spirit. It is the only way, the only way of My constantly coming forth in your life. Let My Word expand and explode into brilliant bloom through you. It shall be. It shall be.

Is it not a better way, to speak My Words continually? So comes the peace and the joy and the strength, strength of purpose and strength of intention. Continue in that strength. Let not up in your intensity. Continue to strengthen your fortress against the enemy with My Words and communion with Me. Study diligently My Word. Meditate on My Word. Your walk in the Spirit shall be perfected. Still yourself before Me. Abide in the Spirit. Continually exercise your spirit by keeping your awareness level always turned toward Me.

Release unto Me your whole being, your whole self. Look not to your own abilities to accomplish that which is before you. Look unto Me for your strength and endurance. My grace is sufficient for you. Many are the words that are spoken by My children in My Kingdom, but words that are spoken through My Spirit carry the creative power to bring them into manifestation for all to see. Speak My Words by My Spirit, for it is those words that are bringing forth My Kingdom. Yea, and those words shall come to pass. Carry on with your labors in My Kingdom. Strike forth along the trail this day with your banner blowing in the breeze. Let your radiance shine. Give forth of yourself. Do not hold back.

Fill your heart with My peace, My joy and My love. Keep it to overflowing at all times, for there will continually be one yearning to know more of Me, that shall be coming to you, to dip into your well of joy, peace and love. That one has come to you from Me. You shall lead them to Me, that they too might be filled with peace, joy and love. You are that watering hole in the oasis, and you are to be overflowing at all times, never caught unawares or unready. You are to be in communion with Me at all times, always ready in due season. A joyful, peaceful heart is a rare thing in this world and easily recognized among the multitudes. You shall stand out and be sought out. Be ready!

Break forth in singing this day, for it is a day of release. It is a day of response to My Word. Release your fears, fear of animosity, fear of judgement by others and fear of repercussions, and the peace that passeth all understanding shall abide within your heart. Rejoice with a new song unto your God. Sing a new song of praise.

You still find your release from tension through eating, instead of through Me. Perfect peace and joy and love drives out tension and gives it no room to grow, just as a healthy stand of grass gives no weeds room to grow. Rest in Me continually. Give tension no place in your life. When the urge to feed your face presents itself, rebuke it, feed your spirit and minister love and praise to Me instead. Your body will shrink, and your spirit will expand. This is no time for resting on your laurels. This is a time for pressing in with all your spirit, soul and body.

Travail is the only way into My Kingdom. Everyone has to start some place. If My Word is not accepted, your prayers of intercession help. You are like an F.B.I. Agent. I give you a job to do and you don't always know what came before or what follows. You simply carry out your task and leave the rest completely in My care. You must be able to dispatch a job and then completely release all back to Me, without retaining any residue of burden. Small residues build up into a heavy load; so unload completely after each job. Resist the temptation to judge. That is My job. Where there is joy and peace, there is no room for a wrong spirit. Break forth this day with a bright spirit. Rejoice and sing like a bird, for the bird sings with joy for the new day and the freedom that that new day promises.

Have you not seen this day the difference between an open spirit and one that is closed to My Spirit? The open spirit absorbs like a sponge, without fear and apprehension. The closed spirit responds with a closed mind and frightened spirit, or else simply a closed, arrogant spirit. The closed spirit has two earmarks: passive assurance and arrogance.

Rejoice, all that live in Zion, for My Spirit shall flow like a river. It shall flow unhindered through and from each of My children. Reach forth your hand and partake of all of the richness of My Kingdom. Leave none of it to rot, unused. Appropriate each blessing in your life to the fullest. Hesitate not to reach for every opportunity and blessing that comes your way, for they are continually coming to you. Blessings are not static. As they are appropriated and passed on, they expand in magnitude. Never allow them to sit idle and stagnate. Be a blessing expander.

Receive your awakening to know more of My will, My Word and My way. My will is made known to My children through obedience. My Word is made known through confident awareness, and My way is made known through My

Word. The study of My Word straight from Scripture is important, so that I may impart to you My wisdom, knowledge and truth directly. Do not neglect this very important channel of blessing. Recite aloud that which is of importance to you. The impact is greater. Do not neglect My Word!

My child, you need not strain or worry about whether or not you are performing in My perfect will. There are within My Kingdom two kinds of people: those who do and those who simply talk about doing; those who believe and put into action and those who simply talk about believing; those who talk about faith and those who step out in faith. Be a doer. True, speaking words of faith and belief inspires people to action, but always "practice what you preach."

Chapter 7

Communion With God

"He wakeneth morning by morning,
He wakeneth mine ear to hear as the learned.
The Lord God hath opened mine ear"
Isaiah 50:4b-5a

Ours is a close communion as between a father and daughter, and you shall continue to rejoice in the freedom and ease of our relationship. Do not forsake your time with Me, for I require devotion in such a relationship. It shall continue to bring overflowing joy to you and bring joy to Me. Rejoice, rejoice, for this is the beginning of an even closer relationship with Me. The meaning of My life here on earth shall become more meaningful to you as you continue to study My Word. You shall witness a great infilling of My Spirit amongst those nearest and dearest to you. It shall be a time of joy and deliverance. Depend not upon your own resources to bring this about. Stand upon the faith that I give to you and let Me bring it about.

Relax and enjoy the time that I have given to you. Redeem the time with faithfulness, but come to Me with a relaxed, joyous heart. Resist the temptation to reject as unworthy time spent quietly and peacefully. Times of tranquility bring peace to the spirit. Many of My children have spent their lives so busy "redeeming the time" that they have never taken the time to get to know Me, to share with Me their time, joys and fellowship. Do not let yourself fall into that rut. Work is un-ending. If you wait until it is done to find the time for Me and My Word and the little joys of life in My Kingdom, you will never find the time to truly have a walk with Me. Do not let work and responsibilities rule you. When you are in the Kingdom, whether your house was perfectly clean or not will have no importance, but if you spent every possible minute learning to know Me better will have every importance. Keep your priorities straight. Reach out and take My hand, and we shall walk through this land victoriously, joyously and forever tuned into life as it should be when My Spirit takes command. That is coming into My rest, letting Me lead the work, letting Me direct the play and the rest.

Take your rest as one who has walked the highways and byways and trod the weary miles. Be not ashamed of spending time quietly without the pressures of tasks crying to be accomplished. Let Me refresh your spirit and your body through this time of peaceful, refreshing solitude and rest. Rest in Me. Enjoy the quiet. Enjoy the smallest of blessings around you. Resist the temptation to lock yourself into one activity after another.

Relate yourself to the situation, but keep your focus ever on Me. Practice makes perfect. Do not regress through lack of alertness. Be on your guard against the status quo. Ever strive for singleness of mind upon Me. Everything else takes care of itself and falls into place as you keep your mind and thoughts focused in My direction. Come to the well often, and drink deeply to maintain your strength and diligence and to know My direction. Maintain a solid foundation by hearing, reading and contemplating My Word. All else is worth nothing without the continual infilling of My Word and continual communion with Me. Everything falls out of synchronization without these two stabilizing forces. Maintain a spirit that is constantly worshiping. Nothing can come against a spirit in worship. Listen, My daughter, for My Word. Keep your spirit constantly tuned to My voice. Learn to recognize it instantly. Keep your focus keen and alert. Remove from you the graveclothes of bondages to anything that draws your awareness away from Me. Proceed with determination to hear My voice, to move with singleness of thought and action.

Ministry is a sacred trust that can only be maintained through constant communion with Me. Constant awareness is the key to constant success. As our communion together wanes, so does all else that is of importance in the life of the Spirit. Constant vigilance that assures a continual focus upon Me in worship and prayer keeps the spirit ever rising to new levels of effectiveness. Know that it is possible for the spirit and mind to be in constant prayer and worship, even while engaging in the affairs of the day. Continually strive for this. Do not let up. Keep your thoughts on Me, and you shall not waver or draw back. Determine your course and stick with it with diligence.

Step up higher into My Kingdom. Do not be satisfied with yesterday's blessings. Appropriate new and more expanded blessings for today and expect even more tomorrow. Step forth over the threshold into a constant state of worship and praise. Keep your eye and your mind and heart's eye continually on Me. Contain not thy spirit. Let it soar in communion and praise with Me.

Be silent, My child, when you would know Me better. You do not come to know another person better by doing all the talking. You come to know him and his inner feelings by listening. Learn to listen quietly. Do not feel that there must always be creative thought put forth by you for there to be prayer. I straighten out the crooked pathways as you keep your focus on Me.

Remain in My love. Remain in the brightness, splendor and immenseness of My love, for it encompasses all creation. It enlarges and grows and totally engrosses those who allow it to grow within them. Once it takes root, it grows, and nothing can stop it. There is no fear within that love. When there is fear, that light has not been allowed to shine, purify, protect and rise above all obstacles. Remain in that love, and all else falls into place.

Be not afraid of solitude, as long as it is spent with Me. Where there is worship, there is joy. The two go hand in hand. So when you say, "Where is the joy?" I say, "Where is the worship?" Harken unto My voice with a constancy that shall seal our relationship with a joy and understanding. Maintain a constant awareness, and I shall lead you in your intercession that it may be pointed and effective. Praise and joy are a natural outflow of a heart filled with love.

Once again the forest was cleared of the slag, and you are free to lift your branches high and soak in the sunshine of My smile. Maintain a constant vigilance. Keep the slag cleared out. Any time your focus keeps being drawn away from Me against your will, know that slag is cropping up and needs to be immediately dealt with and cleared away.

Continue to maintain a vigilance. Know that when the mind tries to take over with, "Why didn't I?" and, "If only" and, "I should have said, or done thus and such," in retrospect, that it is not My Spirit in control, for My Spirit guides and directs at the moment and has no need to look back with regret. My Spirit only looks back with peace and joy and thanksgiving, no matter how the circumstance looks to the naked carnal eye.

Any thought that hovers like a wet blanket to try to smother the Spirit's peace and joy that is constantly your portion must be destroyed by exposing it to My light, which is a consuming fire to all that is not of My Spirit. Speak it forth, lifting it up to Me in relinquishment, and it shall be burned away, leaving only purity and truth. Therefore, languish not under the heavy weight of unrelinquished burdens. Do not hold them to yourself and try to deal with them by yourself. Relinquish all to Me, and let Me carry the weight of the burdens.

The actions of a humble man, a righteous man, are led by Me. When he goes his own way and fails to listen to My leading, but then repents of his wrong actions, I can turn those misdeeds into blessings. To the one with a pliable, humble, repentant spirit everything comes up blessings.

Strike forth along the trail, rejoicing in My care and direct guidance of you. Contain not your exuberance, but let it infect those who come in contact with you this day. There are many in My fold who need your tender loving care. You shall minister to their needs with My love and understanding. Fear not, for the doors shall open as I would have it, and you shall know what is from Me and what is not. You shall know through the leading of My Spirit through you. You shall know by the compassion I shall give you for them. The peace that passeth all understanding is yours through Jesus Christ your Lord. Go in peace and rejoice.

Sing Hallelujah! Sing Hallelujah! Soar forth in newness of life. You are as a newborn child. The newborn is completely trusting, guzzling its food. Its joy is in taking its nourishment and digesting it to the fullest. Rest in Me as a newborn child rests, in complete confidence and trust. Be open and loving with no restraints. Be exceedingly glad. Hallelujah!

Chapter 8

Peace In The Midst Of The Storm

"These things I have spoken unto you, that in Me ye might have peace.
In the world ye shall have tribulation:
but be of good cheer; I have overcome the world."
John 16:33

Are you not My songbird to ring forth the gloriousness of My Kingdom? Let your voice ring forth in joy and praise and richness as like unto My Kingdom. Aside from praising and worshiping Me, there is no greater occupation.

You shall set your foot upon the solid rock and not be swayed. Do you think that I cannot perform that which I have spoken? Yes, I can, and will, that your days may be full to overflowing in the land. Follow your leadings and doubt not, for I am with you. My rod and My staff, they comfort you, and you shall know peace and understanding and joy all the days of your life, and you shall dwell in the House of the Lord forever. Be not overshadowed by thoughts of the carnal mind, but overcome them by thoughts of Me. So shall you know the sweetness of victory, and so shall we rejoice together in everlasting song.

I go before you in all matters. I make the crooked straight. Do not become despondent or impatient. Rely on My perfect timing, and do not despair or wonder. What I have begun, I will complete. Rest in the light, joy and radiance of My smile.

Praise My Holy Name. Step forth with gladness of heart, for My ways are everlasting and full of meaning to the one who embraces them. Embrace them with your whole heart. Stray not away from My love, but constantly be aware of it. Constantly be aware of My Presence and leading in your life. Rejoice, for your life is in My hand forever, and your steps are led, guided and directed by Me. Walk in faith, knowing this. Sow your seed with jubilant abandon. You will sow seed you are not even aware of sowing.

Reach forth day-by-day and appropriate those things that I deem necessary for your growth. Embrace them with your whole heart. They are there for you day-by-day, not every other day or every third day. Every day needs My nourishment to make it complete and lacking in nothing. Consider My Son. He drew apart at night and did without sleep to fulfill this need. You are in greater need. Do not let your spirit starve through neglect.

Go on into maturity. Strive not to measure your life against others. I have given you a walk with Me unique unto itself, just as all of My creations are unique and different from every other. So, too, is your walk with Me. I will lead you into experiences that will have no road map of others' lives to go by, so don't seek for the security of a road map. Learn to love and enjoy the beauty of a jagged crag, the beauty of unexplored territory. Claim that territory for Me and go on. Relinquish unto Me all fears of the unknown. My children must be free to move unbound by convention, loosed from fear of the unknown and aware of who they are, My Ambassadors. Be released from the pressures that have beset you from within and from without.

My Word is as a gurgling brook in a dry oasis. It brings joy and peace to the soul. Do not stray from that brook of living water. Be always ready to give others a refreshing drink of that fresh brook water. Amongst all My treasures you will find Me. My treasures are My people, for they bring Me joy.

Haste not to bring forth that which I have for you. Allow the preparation time to be complete, that you might step out on a firm and unmoved foundation. Patience is indeed a virtue. Patience and faith linked together form a bond that cannot be broken. Therein is strength. Walk in that strength unhesitatingly, looking not back but ever forward. Rejoice in the now, for the now includes the reality of those things believed for, those things unseen that are yours in the Spirit. Walk as a horse with blinders on to see where you are and where you are going but not be distracted by where you have been and what is trying to distract you from the left and right. My child, I will lead you through all kinds of terrain, but My guiding hand will always bring you through. You will only stumble if you look back, for then you will lose sight of My guiding light up front. Hurt feelings come from looking back. In continually looking forward, all things are continually new. All relationships are continually new and fresh if you don't ever look back to drag along old responses. If you don't look back, you can see each person as I, the Lord, see them, and respond to them as I, the Lord, respond to them, innocent and pure, because I, the Lord, died to make them so.

You have found yourself walking a winding path, leading around the same lake of muck and mire. Look not at the muck and mire as though captivated by it. Turn your back upon it, and look not again upon it. Set your feet in the path that leads straightway from it, with your faith set upon Me, your eyes set upon Me and your ears set upon My Word. Be not held down by the activities and thoughts of the mind. Be

set free as My songbird, to soar in the Spirit, no longer held in
bondage to that level of learning that shall propel you ever
higher. You are healed and will remain healed. Stand in My
Word, and the power thereof, and nothing can hold you; no
confusion, mixed emotions, frustrations or fear can slow your
walk with Me. There is a time and a season for all things. My
time, of this you are learning.

Learning to be still from within and without will cause
less waste in your life, less dissipated energy, and you will become stronger in mind, body and spirit. There will be a reservoir within your spirit that will not only feed you but also
will be enough for all around you that wish to drink of the fruit
of the vine, the flow of My Spirit into you and from you, the
river of living water. But you must drink deep and often, that
your reservoir may never be drained or low but filled to overflowing. Today, you quieted yourself and drank deeply. This
do constantly. Now move out in the natural course of action
befitting the day, taking one task at a time. Lay a course of action, and the results will follow. There will be no frustration or
confusion if you set out first things first, not being pushed or
pressured by the force of time or outside indirection. Set your
course, stick to it, and do not let the foxes harass you by their
begging and whelping. Do this, and your course will become
more clear and sure. Do it My way, not yours, for I do not desire My little children to be caught up in hailstorms blown this
way and that way, beaten and bruised and hurt by this battling
against them. I would have My children be as young saplings
along the riverbank, with their roots going down deep and
strong to drink and draw deeply the living waters, firmly
planted, immovable, able to sway and bend with the storm, de-
flecting the power and force thereof. They will be left standing
erect, steady and strong, but ever so flexible and pliable in the
gentle breeze of My Spirit. This storm through which you have
just passed was intended by the enemy to uproot you and

break you. You have remained standing and steadfast, but badly bruised. My healing is with you. Worry not, for you resisted well and shall remain flexible and sway to the gentle moving of My Spirit.

There shall come upon you a new radiance from above. It shall shine like the morning sun. My ways shall become more and more your ways, and you shall know the peace, the joy and the contentment of the salvation of your Lord. Unto them who heed My voice, the reward is great. Cast all of your cares upon Me, for I love you. I am your burden bearer. Many are the trials of this world, but you simply move through them knowing that I am your strength and your shield. Strength comes through encounter, and faith comes through battles won. Rejoice, and be mightily glad, for ours is the victory, always!

Rest in My love. The ways of My Spirit unfold as a flower, one petal at a time. First the outer petals unfold, and then the inner petals of inner beauty and strength. Rest in the strength of My love, for one petal at a time My attributes become your attributes. The tides come in, and the tides go out, but no erosion takes place that isn't led by My hand to mold into perfection those who love Me.

Refer not back to days of old. It is a new day. All things are new to them who love the Lord. The Lord is your strength and your song, a present help in times of need. Say to yourself, "Never again shall I look back with regret or with mourning, for all things work together for good to those who love the Lord." Your comings in and your goings out are all known to Me and are in My hand. Tarry not with old regrets and hurts. Give them to Me and rejoice, for I shall turn your sorrows to great joy. Rejoice and be glad, for I am with you always.

Draw not back from days of trials and struggles. Encounter them with singleness of purpose, that you might be strengthened. March on victoriously, knowing that the foe has been met, the battle has been won and that the reward has been great. "No encounters" means "status quo," and "status quo" means the opposite of growth and life. It means stagnation and death. So do not be afraid of encounters. Rejoice in them. Keep your eyes on Me, and walk through the land as I guide. Each encounter is a beautiful package, a present from Me, no matter how it looks on the outside. The struggle is getting through the outer covering to the beauty that lies inside. Be steadfast. Do not give up. Rejoice in the now.

The peace that passeth all understanding shall fill your heart and mind this day, for you have come to the well of forgiveness, repentance and love, and you have been heard. I do respond with haste to those who come with repentance, love and faith.

Blessed is the one who knows My will and performs it. Blessed is the one who steadfastly looks to Me in all things. There is a time and a place for all things. Of My times and of My place you are learning. "Not by power, not by might, but by My Spirit," saith the Lord. Walk steadfastly by My side and all things shall come to pass as I have ordained. Rest in your redemption, for it is lacking in nothing. The end is complete. It can be trusted. I can be trusted. Maintain a constant assurance of this fact. Remove from you any doubt or hesitancy to rely completely on Me. Keep your eyes looking upward, and rejoice!

Chapter 9

Run The Good Race To Victory

"Wherefore, seeing we also are compassed about
with so great a cloud of witnesses, let us lay aside every weight,
and the sin which doth so easily beset us,
and let us run with patience the race that is set before us."
Hebrews 12:1

My peace I give unto you; not as the world gives peace, but a peace beyond measure. Maintain your stride, knowing that I run beside you through the day.

My peace that passeth all understanding is yours today, for you have passed through the door of understanding into the workings of My Spirit. There are times of trial and of sorrow, but they are meant to strengthen and sustain your spirit. Know that I have My faithful ones standing watch in prayer, with diligence, to help carry you through to victory. They, too, are strengthened through participation in the struggle to reach the victory, to gain the prize in the ever upward calling of the Lord Jesus Christ. To Him be the glory and honor forever and ever.

The fear of failure before the Lord is sin. I delight in the perfect trust of My children. Remain serenely in My hands, knowing that I am always in control. The joy of the Lord is your strength!

Restitution shall be made. Restitution shall come your way. Just as with Job, I break, but I restore again and My restoration is always greater than the original. Job learned trust, patience and perseverance, and so have you. Rejoice, for the time of restoration is near.

As sure as the sun shines in the day and the stars come out at night, I bless those who bless My Name. Be strong, firm and courageous in spirit, soul and body for I am with you always to sustain you and go before you. Faint not, but strive ever forward. Rejoice, and be of good cheer, for all is in My hand.

Run the good race. Be persistent and relentless. When the victory is won, do not retreat and rest. That is the time to press ever onward so that you don't lose ground but continue to gain. It is a constant state of gaining the victory, maintaining the victory and gaining new ground. Remain steadfast and sure.

Run the good race. Finish the course with honor. Persistence and determination keep one ever striving upward and onward, with the eyes and spirit ever looking upward to Christ. Persist. Relinquish not nor draw back, but be ever moving forward. Meditation, prayer, thanksgiving and praise are the wheels that propel My children ever onward and upward. Keep those wheels well greased and in constant motion. Turn not the wheel to the right or the left, but straight forward.

Win the good race. It takes steadiness, uprightness, stamina, fitness, purity, determination, perseverance, strength and soundness. They become their own rewards of steadiness, uprightness, stamina, fitness, purity, determination, perseverance, strength, and soundness.

Continue the good race, and know the joy of your salvation, the peace and the knowledge of My will being performed in and through your life.

My ways are perfect. So shall your ways be perfect, for does My Word not say, "Be ye perfect even as I am perfect?" Resist the enemy, and he shall flee from you. Keep a tender spirit, alert to My slightest nudge. I shall lead. I shall lead, even as I have done in the past. You can be assured of that leading and rely upon it. My ways shall never fail. They bring life, joy and peace. Continue on! Continue on!

I, the Lord, your God, go before you in all that you do. Be not distressed nor discouraged, for nothing shall fail to come to pass as I have said. Press ever onward, for I, the captain of your faith, go ever before you and will never fail you. Ours is the victory! Ours is the victory!

All shall be done as I have said. Have you not come out of Egypt, dwelt in the wilderness for 40 months and come into the land of plenty, and have I not led and cleared the way? My hand of deliverance has not been shortened, and you shall find that I shall refresh and re-establish those who have lost the freshness of their first love. Joy and radiance shall be returned to them. They shall know whereof they have trodden and from whence comes true peace, joy and freedom of spirit, for I shall renew their spirits in truth and strength. Rejoice, for the time is near that all shall know from whence cometh your joy, strength and endurance. My truth shall stand and show forth deliverance.

As the sheaves of barley are reaped in due season, so, too, all things and events of My Kingdom come to pass in due season. Can you make the grain grow by your own efforts? No, they grow by My timetable, by My hand. Worry not as to the season. It will be there, and you will be there, and you will know that it is time to harvest. You cannot help to birth a chicken from its egg. It would die. It must come in due season. Of My times and My seasons you truly are learning, uppermost being patience, forgiveness, trust and love, as I have said. Rest now, for all is in My hand. Not a single grain will fall to the ground prematurely and die before harvest. The harvest shall be full. Trust Me. Rely on My steadfastness. We shall prevail. We shall prevail. It shall be. It shall be.

The seasons change, and so do My dealings with My people take on new depth and meaning. There shall be new awakenings within your spirit, and you shall know from whence cometh those stirrings. Greet them with enthusiasm and joy, for My blessings are upon you to show you the way out of the valleys and ravines and into the magnitude of the heights of My Spirit. There is joy in My heart for you, for you have not forsaken My commandment to love one another as I have loved you. Continue on! Continue on!

Receive your just reward. Receive the bounty of your labor. Rejoice, for into your hand have I placed the desires of your heart. Surely it is a time for rejoicing, for all shall know that mighty are My ways and nothing shall stand before Me. Victory is sweet, and ours is the victory. Jericho's walls have truly fallen.

Sing as a bird. A bird does not sing for love and approval. It sings for the pure joy of singing, for the pure joy of being a part of My creation. Therefore, the joy and beauty of My creation pours through it. Thus will you now truly sing as My songbird, for the pure joy of My love within you and for the pure joy of being mine. Therefore, that pure joy and love will pour through you and others will seek that joy of being Mine too. You shall find My praises flowing from your lips as the waterfall, to water a dry and thirsty land. In perfect trust, you shall sing forth My praises. Take a lesson from the birds. Continually sing My praises. Then you will always be prepared.

Establish a rapport between thee and thy brethren. Rush not to instill within them the knowledge of My ways. Instead, open avenues of identity and trust. My Spirit shall move and prepare the way. Haste not! Haste not, but be open to avenues as they are opened before you.

Fear Not

"There is no fear in love; but perfect love casteth out fear:
because fear hath torment. He that feareth is not made perfect in love.
We love Him because He first loved us."
1 John 4:18-19

Release unto Me your fears, fear of reproach, fear of failure and fear of misunderstanding. Lay them all upon the altar before Me this day, that they not be a stumbling block to you ever again. So be it!

Take care of yourself. Nurture the warmth of My Spirit within, that others might be warmed from its warmth. Don't let yourself doubt, for you have My wisdom and persistence within. Stand firmly planted, with your feet apart and your hands on your hips. There will always be those who think you are wrong. The slings and the arrows will fly, but they can never penetrate, for you wear My armor of protection. They will come from those who know themselves, but you know Me.

Fear not My child, for I have all things in hand. Your comings in and your goings out are all known to Me. You dwell in the shadow of My wing and I will never forsake you. When adversity comes, it is only for a season, to teach you strength, trust, reliance and steadfastness. Stumble not and faint not, for there is always an end to all things. Joy replaces sorrow and rejoicing replaces trials. Enter into the joy of your salvation, and look not back to the trials of yesterday. Always look upward and onward. Rejoice daily at the new things I send your way taking one at a time in stride. Do not get bogged down, but keep a steady rhythm of activity. Remember to keep your words few and your prayers many.

Have I not told you that I will provide all that you need for physical, mental and spiritual growth? In the end, nothing will be found wanting or missing. Resist the enemy, and he shall flee from you. Hesitate not to rebuke and refuse that which is not from Me. There will be times when it would seem that I have forsaken you, but I have not. Hold on with trust and reliance, and you will see that these times are blessings in disguise. Rejoice evermore. Never give up. Know that one way or another the victory is always ours.

My child, My child, why do you languish? Come up higher, and come up out of the muck and mire of the soul and mind. Do you not know the joys of the heights? Why stay bogged down in the lowlands of the heart, soul and spirit? Soar once again.

Stand guard upon the high tower of your soul, that no foul thing might overcome and enter. Be ever on watch, to guard against error or neglect of being obedient, against pride or false humility. Be honest in all things: no false fronts or faces; everything up front and as is. Stand firm in My Word and in the Glory of that Word, that My Glory might continue to shine about you. Stand fast! Stand fast! Let not up, for the Glory of the Lord is your strength. Hallelujah! Hallelujah! Rejoice, for that Glory and strength are yours in abundance.

There is peace in knowing that My will pours forth as streams of living water to those who would but accept it.

There is no need for apprehension, fear or rebuke when one trusts Me to bring about My perfect will. It will come about. Do what you can in the time allotted. Then rest in perfect peace, knowing that I have undertaken and all will be taken care of as it should be. Rejoice in My perfect care and provision. Be refreshed this day as you take one thing at a time, relaxed and at perfect peace.

My little children frolic and play in the sunshine, but there are days of rain when they must stay inside with their noses against the window pane, patiently waiting again for the sun to shine. There must be both: the more confined days, with hope for the future, and the days of joyful activity. Learn to enjoy both. Do not regard one over the other, for they both have their place. Go forth now with a song in your heart, refreshed and revived.

Discipline comes forth as one heeds My Word. As one becomes knowledgeable in My Word, one comes to know that I am victorious. If I live in you and you live in Me, then I, in you, am victorious and the victory is ours. Hang on to this. Believe it, and live it.

Enter in with joy this day, for this day marks the beginning of a new phase in your life. You have walked out from under the shadows, into the light. You shall feel the warmth of the rays of that light infilling your whole being, and there shall come a new peace and assurance to your heart. You shall know as never before that I am in complete control of your life and the lives of those you love. My hand is not shortened. It is reached out to you with love and affection, for you have walked the highways and the byways and have come through to the light. Bask in the warmth of that light which is My light, the light of My smile. Rejoice, rejoice, rejoice! Break forth in singing and praise.

Rise up, 0 Daughter of Zion, and follow Me. Look neither to the right nor left, but follow straightway after Me. Your
path goes up and down as rolling hills, but your path is
straight as laid out by Me. Joyfully skip along that path, singing praises, for My light shines along that path, sparkling and
radiant. Your destination is sure and visible in the distance.
Keep your eye steady. We shall prevail!

Rejoice, for the work that is taking place in your life, for
the restoration that I am working in your life. Be not afraid of
"your own thoughts" for they are My thoughts within you. I
am restoring your joy, peace, trust and faith in a new and more
expanded way. I am building your life, stone-on-stone, with a
strength that cannot be toppled. Each stone bears My Name
and My Being within it, My perfectness and completeness. So
wrestle not with the uncertainty that you feel, but rejoice in the
knowledge that each stone is being placed one-by-one as I
would have it. Hallelujah! A might fortress is your God, and a
mighty fortress am I making of you.

My arm shall be strong on your behalf. I shall lift you
up, high above the tempest, and they who see shall know that I
am Lord. Surely goodness and mercy shall follow you all the
days of your life, and you shall dwell in the house of the Lord
forever. Liken not what you saw yesterday to what you shall
see tomorrow. Do not expect the new to be as the old. Expect a
new and perfect thing in your life constantly. Your life shall be
as that of My son, Peter, who said, "Bid me to walk on the water," and he did. But because of the faith and trust that I have
wrought in your life, you shall not look down at the tempest all
around you. You shall look up and rejoice and know that I am
Lord of all. My will reigns, and you shall not be disappointed.
You shall walk unfalteringly upon the water. So it shall be. So
be not afraid when the waves swirl all around you, for you will
find sure footing all along your pathway. And worry not as to
where you will find that sure footing. Just know that each time

you put your foot down, just as each time you take a breath, it will find its ultimate destination smoothly, and any unnecessary action or effect will disappear, just as when one exhales in breathing. So step out, one step at a time, knowing that each step is as a stone being laid upon the foundation of My Kingdom within you which cannot be shaken. Strength is a by-word in My Kingdom, and you are strong in My sight. Go forth in strength. Go forth in peace, and go forth with the assurance of My Word, for it is a lamp unto your feet and a road map along your path. Go forth with joy.

Say not unto yourself, "I have arrived," for in this journey on earth you never arrive. It is a continual, "I am arriving." Keep a continual vigilance upon your heart to say, "The Lord, my God, is in command. Nothing shall miss His eye. Nothing shall lack His touch." I am restoring to My people the firm and unmovable knowing of My moving in their behalf to heal them in body, soul, mind and spirit. I am restoring to them the joy of their salvation. Maintain a stout vigilance on your heart. Let not the doubts come in. Rebuke them at the beginning, and do not let them enter. Rejoice, for I know your weaknesses and stand ready to sustain you in them, to make you strong where you once were weak. So, take up your bed, and walk. Walk strong and tall, for I, your God, am with you.

Fear not, My little one. Gird yourself, and stand ready to march. Stand ready and prepared to march at My command. Strengthen yourself. Prepare. David girded himself and slew Goliath. We, too, shall kill Goliath. The prayers of others have paved the way to victory. A little one shall lead them. Fear not, but stand prepared. Stay in My Word. Keep your heart attuned to My Word. Resist the enemy, and keep your heart at peace and full of joy. I shall sustain you and uphold you. Say not in your heart, "It is no use," but say in your heart, "Great is your faithfulness, Lord, unto Me. All that I have, your hand has provided. Great is your faithfulness, Lord, unto me." We shall prevail.

The classroom of life is always on the move. A little of this and a little of that all combine together to make the whole. Despise not the seemingly insignificant parts, for what seems insignificant can many times be the kingpin or key part. Take each day in stride, as allotted, with praise and thanksgiving. Restore joy, when depleted, by singing My praises. Resent not the small inconveniences that arise, but see them as open doors in another direction. There are no vacuums or empty spaces in My Kingdom. All things work together to form the whole. Be at peace, and rejoice!

Rise up and sing in the spirit. Broadcast the radiance of My Spirit upon you. Let the sunshine of My radiance shine forth. Rejoice and be glad, for I shall show you many things that you have not been aware of before. They shall be as gifts from Heaven. Now, rejoice. Let My praises resound in your heart, and let thanksgiving come forth from your lips, for I do all things well, and you are My handiwork. I shall not let you down. Go forth this day with new resolve and strength, perseverance and determination, to walk in My paths of purpose and joy. Hallelujah!

Chapter 11

Rest In My Love

"I have set the Lord always before me:
because He is at my right hand, I shall not be moved.
Therefore my heart is glad, and my glory rejoiceth:
my flesh also shall rest in hope."
Psalms 16:8-9

Strengthen your girdle about you, and stand tall and strong that you stumble not nor slip. Restrain from added burdens. Do not take on the added weight. It is a time for stabilizing and strengthening from within, of strengthening your position and the foundation upon which your whole family sits. Unity and oneness shall come forth in abundance, and you all shall rejoice. Partake of the freshness of the breeze that blows through the oasis. Partake of the reality of wholeness coming forth in each one. Rejoice! Rejoice! Rejoice!

Happy is the one who trusts in and truly relies on My leadings, for he shall feed peacefully on the dew-laden, tender grasses each morning and be at peace the rest of the day. Allay your self styled worries and anxieties. Once again, be My sheep who perfectly trusts in My guiding and protecting hand. Let Me bring things about, and do not fret in the meantime. Stand tall in My Spirit!

There is a time and a season for all things. Among My steadfastly faithful ones, I do send seasons of rest and contemplation, seasons of refreshing and strengthening. You shall come forth stronger in your resolve to serve Me, to trust Me and to love Me and appreciate My guiding hand with you and those you love. Do not hesitate to seek My guidance, no matter how trivial the situation may seem. Spread your wings. Enlarge the place of your tent. The latter days will not be as the former days. I am strengthening and expanding your life. Expand, expand, and rejoice, for the expansion is built on a strong foundation and cannot be toppled. Refrain from speaking of what was. Live and concentrate on the present and what I am doing in you now. Keep your eyes fixed on Me in the now. Maintain that quiet assurance that I am with thee and thine forever.

Expand the awareness of My Presence and guiding hand in your life. Expand your base of reaching out to Me and appropriation. Stretch forth your wings into greater heights of glory in My Name. Make every breath to be a praise to My Name. Rejoice at My coming in you.

Trust in Me with all your heart, and lean not unto your own understanding. Revealed step-by-step shall be My plan for you, and you shall know as each piece falls into place with perfect precision and grace. Revealed shall be the plan of the ages in your life and that of your loved one. Hesitate not to trust and obey and rejoice in the ever unfolding plan, for My mercies do endure forever, and My blessings do go forth to those who love Me and unto their generations. Blessed are the meek, for they shall see Heaven, and blessed are the upright in heart, for they shall see God.

Strengthen your steps through exercising this day in body and spirit. Prepare to step out in My Name with stamina and strength of body, soul and spirit. Prepare a way for Me in the wilderness. Resist the enemy, and he shall flee from you. Rely upon My guiding hand at all times. We shall strike forth upon an unmarked trail in the wilderness. You shall need My guidance for each step. Others shall follow to make it a well marked trail, deeply imprinted across the wilderness. The pathway is narrow but straight and leads to My Kingdom and the fullness thereof. Rejoice and be mightily glad, for ours is the glory in victory and ours is the joy in completeness. Strike forth this day with pleasure in your bones and rejoicing in your heart, for you shall see visions of righteousness, of peace and joy and wholeness in mind, body, soul and spirit. Now go your way with rejoicing!

My beloved sings a song of praise. It is sweetness to My ears. Songs of joy and praise are like a beautiful raiment upon those from whose lips it proceeds. It is a raiment of protection and warmth and radiates My light and peace. Wear it perpetually. Be forever warmed by its radiation, and let others be warmed by the radiated light and warmth that shines forth. It warms the innermost being and brings hope to those who were chilled. It is like a warm blanket to those who have been out in the storms of life, and leads them to Me.

I make of your heart a garden growing with beautiful flowers and growing things. My Word keeps it watered with the living and rejuvenating water of life. The more care you give it the more it produces. Ours shall be a fruitful garden. Bring forth from the garden of your heart the wisdom which is Mine. Ponder it. Handle it from every side, and let it work its weight of gold in your heart and whole being. Respect the feelings of others, but move not from that strong foundation.

The grass often seems greener on the other side, but bloom where I have planted you, for there the soil is perfectly mixed for your growth. Rejoice, for I am cultivating, feeding and watering the plot in which you reside, daily and faithfully. You shall be a beautiful flower, for I do all things well.

The days of fruitfulness have begun. They shall start slowly and gain momentum. Keep your heart attuned to Mine, that I might continue to lead and guide each step. The fruits of our labor shall be many, and they shall produce wholesome fruit, sweet to the taste. Your labors shall not be in vain. Rejoice in the warmth of My smile. The days shall follow one upon the other, rich in My Word and filled with and by My Blessing Spirit. Step-by-step, proceed. I shall lead you, and you shall know as each step approaches. Sing with joy as you go, and let your joy shine forth to all you meet along the way. Proceed with gladness.

My sheep shall hear My voice, and My sheep shall know My voice. Should you not be one to lead them to the hearing and knowing of My voice, and does this not come about through praising and singing praises to Me? Sing forth My praises with merriment and joy. Sing forth My praises with warmth and deepness of heart. Sing forth My praises with reverence and awe. My children shall know Me and know that I speak to them on a one-to-one basis. Rejoice and be glad, for you shall shine forth as a beacon. Light the way to My Presence, through praise and rejoicing in Me. Sing Hallelujahs, sing Hosannas, and sing Amens, for I shall be in your singing and with you to accomplish all that I have laid before you.

Go forth this day with My Spirit upon you. Strive not; simply be. Show forth My loving kindness and joyfulness. Show forth My compassion and straightforwardness. Show forth My meekness and love.

You shall be strong. You shall take hold of My strength and prevail. Blessed is the one who relies not on his own strength but knows how to draw on My strength, for only My strength is sufficient to succeed. Rely on Me to hold you up. Rely on Me to restore and supply all that you need. Rejoice and be glad, for we shall prevail. I have ordained it, and it shall come to pass. The Glory of the Lord shall shine about you and give you peace.

Hold fast to and cleave to My Word. Rely on My Word to hold you up. It is a strong bulwark against all that would come against you. Receive My Spirit in its fullness. My Spirit descends upon you as a dove of peace. Fill your heart with My Words and My peace, for I am your uplifter, protector and guide, and I shall be with you and in you to fulfill and bring forth that which I have ordained and planned for you. Rejoice and look up, for I shall lead you every step of the way.

Have you not seen this day that My Spirit moves through many channels to bring you in line with My perfect will? Hasten not to proclaim all that I have given you from the housetops. My ways and My Spirit are swallowed and absorbed by small mouthfuls. Remain steadfastly open and alert to My leading, and all shall go smoothly and well. Hasten not to run ahead of Me. We shall plod step-by-step, and each step shall be received and accepted with joy and love. Continue on. Continue on. It shall all fall into place, and you shall know that it is as I would have it. Fill your heart with My Words and My peace, for I am your uplifter, protector and guide, and I shall be with you and in you to fulfill and bring forth that which I have ordained and planned for you. Rejoice and look up, for I shall lead you every step of the way.

Harken unto My voice more closely and with greater regularity, for I have much to show you, to share with you and to teach you. Come into the Holy of Holies with persistence and purposefulness of heart. Knock and keep on knocking, for I am the rewarder of those who persist and do not give up. Rays of light shine forth as the noonday sun from those who seek Me diligently, for My Presence becomes ever stronger in their lives and My Glory shines ever brighter from them. They are My strong ones, and they cannot be moved, for they know in whom they believe and are persuaded that nothing can sway them from their divinely inspired course. Be one of My stalwart ones that shine and blaze forth brightly, ever brighter and brighter. We shall go from Glory-to-Glory and nothing shall stop us.

Come forth! Come forth, I say, with newness of life and heart peace which is evident to all. I restore unto you a newness of joy in your salvation and an assurance of My provision in all things, which grows stronger each day. Blessings be to you, My child, and to your household. Rise up in your spirit, and shine forth My radiance.

Continue to cast your lot with Me, and I shall show you vistas that you have not dreamed of and blessings immeasurable. My children are blessed abundantly and know from whence cometh those blessings. Remain in My care, and rejoice and sing with joy, for My little ones enjoy the oneness and nearness and protection of My everlasting love.

Go forth this day, armed with My Word as your protection and your guide. Go forth, armed with the knowledge that I am in you and work through you to bring forth My perfect will in you and those around you whom you love. I will never leave you nor forsake you. I know your weaknesses and strengthen you in those weak areas, so that you might come up strong and lacking in nothing. The evil one cannot touch you as long as you stand faithful and true to My Word, as long as I abide in you and you abide in Me. Stand strong, stand true, and stand with determination to do My will. We shall prevail. We shall prevail, and all shall know that I am, and that I am the rewarder of those who diligently seek Me.

Chapter 12

Be My Praise

*"I will praise thee, O Lord, with my whole heart;
I will show forth all thy marvelous works.
I will be glad and rejoice in thee:
I will sing praise to thy name, O thou Most High."*
Psalms 9:1-2

Shine forth! Shine forth, and radiate My Glory and power to others. Let it fall as the mist of rain upon them, and they shall receive. Rejoice, for My Spirit does shine forth from you.

Stretch forth your wings, and fly with abandon, for I am the undergirding strength that guides and sustains you. Fly with joy and freedom, unafraid. Soar with delight, and marvel at the freedom of flight that is possible when one lets go and trusts My undergirding strength. Try it. You'll like it. It is like being an eagle who can simply soar and glide and do anything in flight, because I, your Lord, am in, through and under you. I give the strength, protection, guidance and all that is needed so that there is no fear, apprehension, anxiety or concern, just freedom of flight and the exhilaration of that freedom. What rest, what freedom, what serenity, what confidence and what trust comes from a complete letting go of burdens and a total reliance on Me. So are you to sing and live your life as that soaring bird, for you are My songbird and you are to sing and live and dwell in perfect freedom and trust and reliance in Me, for I shall never, no never, no never leave you nor forsake you, nor let you down. Let us continue from this day forward in perfect unity and oneness. You are My songbird, but I am your underlying, sustaining and strengthening power. Rely totally on Me! Depend totally on Me! I shall never disappoint you. Spend much time in flight!

Praise pours forth from My children as water poured from from the rock in Moses' time, when they are in perfect fellowship with Me. Keep the garden I have given you well watered with praise and thanksgiving. My peace is upon you, is in you and through you, and you shall know in ways beyond your understanding how deep that peace runs like a river within you. Do not doubt. Know that it is so. Rest in that peace. Let your life continue to be carried along by that peace. It will not fail you or let you down, for that peace is Christ Jesus.

Keep your hope and faith in Me strong. Let not up. Do not let your mind toy with doubt. Refuse it at every turn. Rebuke it, and turn from it. Of such is My Kingdom built, a strong faith and trust in Me.

There shall come a day when you shall say, "I have no part in this." But I shall say to you, "Heed well My Words," for they shall hold you steady in the water, and you shall not drown. You shall ride along on the gentle breeze of My Spirit to safety. Remain quiet in your spirit, for it is a time of strengthening and growth. Time enough to move out as I would have it. Rejoice that I have rooted out the roadblocks. Move on, day-by-day, as we steadily progress together, hand in hand. Continue on! Continue on!

Come alert in the spirit. Receive My Spirit of alertness and praise. Release unto Me the spirit of lethargy. Now let's get on with the day with the spirit of rejoicing.

Resist the temptation to run when you do not understand the situation. Stand your ground and wait for My light, revelation and wisdom to shine upon the situation. Stand in expectation, expecting Me to act with decision. My truth shall always win. I shall never leave you nor forsake you. Stand firm your ground. Be still, and know that I am God. I love you and rejoice in you.

My Word reaches far beyond the moment it is spoken. It is like a pebble thrown in the water that ripples out in circles, endlessly. My Word shimmers like diamonds, like the sun shimmering on the water as it ripples. Reach out your hand, and continue to give forth My Word to a hungry world, as I lead. They will come to you in abundance. Be ready to give forth of the Water of Life.

Start in the Old Testament, and work your way forward. You will find the food which you are seeking. My Word is a whole and is to be taken as a whole. It is a well-rounded diet. Leave your reservations behind, and come into My Word, "whole hog." Come to My Word with expectations, with high expectations of a grand feast, for that it shall be. Bon Appetit! With love, Jesus!

Stick close to home and perform your duties, the little jobs that have been waiting patiently for attention. For do you not know that it is each little job done with precision and faithfulness that brings to completion the whole? Let your heart sing as you work. Let your spirit rejoice as it works in partnership with Me this day. Your spirit, motivated and led by Mine, can accomplish many things with ease and adeptness. This day you shall see how we can work as one in the Spirit. Stay keenly alert and responsive, and rejoice with lighthearted joy. Let us proceed.

Proceed with faith this day. Know for a fact that I am leading and guiding you, and give no attention to anything that would say otherwise. Walk in the strength and assurance and fortitude that I have given and rejoice.

Continue on as you have My child, speaking My Word, doing My Word, living My Word and being My Word. Respond to the nudgings I give without fear or doubt, for I will carry you through each and every time. Carry on. Carry on.

Tie your shoelaces, that you trip not on the unimportant. The dangling shoelaces are as dangling burdens, cares and details of everyday life. Keep them continually tied in neat bows, lying at My feet. Only when you allow them to become untied and dangle in disarray can you trip and fall over them and become entangled. My peace lies in an ordered life whose focus is on Me. As long as the details of everyday life are tied in bows before My Presence, the spirit is free to soar and fly with Me. Done in reverse, the spirit is tied, and the natural life lies in disarray and confusion.

Proceed, as I lead. Be not afraid to share of the fullness of My Spirit, for each seed shall grow and multiply. My Spirit is victorious. What is given by the Spirit is received by the spirit. Therein lies success. Be My Spirit, and others will receive and be My Spirit. Be My joy, and others will receive and be My joy. Be My love, and others will receive and be My love. Be My peace, and others will receive and be My peace. Be not these things and others whom I have given you will neither be these things. That is what the Scripture means when it says to whom much is given, there lies the greater responsibility.

Much more is expected, but it all comes about naturally through being, receiving, giving and focusing totally on Me. Live through My Spirit, and you will exude My Spirit in all that you say and do. Then, everything comes up victory.

Man does not live by bread alone, but by every word that proceedeth from the mouth of God. Feed on those words and become strong and resilient. Press on to know My Word, that it be a part of you as surely as each breath you take is a part of you. Relax your hold on life, and let Me hold on for you. Remain in My love. Stray not from underneath the protective covering of My love for you. Be refreshed this day. Let Me open and shut doors for you. Let Me show you My love for you. Relax and follow Me. I go before you, clearing the way and strengthening you as we go. Rejoice and be glad. Ours is the victory every time. Radiate this day with My love and laughter.

Light thy lamp, that it may shine even brighter through thanksgiving and praise. Rise in your spirit to meet Me in ever higher realms of joy. Rejoice at the ever broadening scope before us. Let Me pour out My Spirit upon you in an even greater measure that shall bring greater peace and joy to thee and to Me.

You will know what it means to praise Me with your whole heart, and it will be glorious for you and for Me. You will rise into realms that you have never heretofore imagined or known. Respond as My heart touches your heart. Be alert and ready. Kindle the fires, that they diminish not in intensity. Make ready the way of the Lord.

You are to be cool, laid back and confident of My protection and care for you and everything you own. Being uptight is not of Me. It comes from the enemy. Refuse to listen to

him. Nothing escapes My watchful eye. Nothing can evade
My control. I am strong and faithful unto those who have
called upon Me, and you have called upon Me. Refuse to be
upset. Whatever has been safely placed in My hands can and
should remain there. Do not rebuke yourself for having not
taken it back unto yourself for your supervision. That it fool-
ishness.

Wrestle not with yourself. Rest in My continued grace
and protection from failure and rebuke. I shall keep you always within the limits of My will for you, always well within
those limits. So worry not but rejoice and sing, for ours is the
victory. We have faced the enemy, and we have prevailed, and
we shall continue to prevail.

Raise up your heart in praise to Me this day. Rejoice in
your deliverance and security in My love and protection over
you and yours. Your days are numbered with the very elect,
for you shall continue to praise and give thanks in My Name.
My Glory shines forth from those who love Me, and My love
and protection are theirs forever. Shine forth My light this day.
Reverberate My praises and rejoice. Speak to Me with words of
love. Speak to Me with words of praise. I shall lift you up and
uphold you and love you with an unending love. Proceed this
day with joy in your heart. We shall be delighted together.

Chapter 13

Stay Free

"And ye shall know the truth, and the truth shall make you free."
John 8:32

I bestow blessings on My children in abundance. I show mercy and love that cannot be measured. Blessed is he who cometh in the name of the Lord. His days cannot be numbered as the world numbers days, for his days are blessed beyond degree. Rejoice little blessed one, and walk tall in My Spirit.

Lean not unto your own understanding, but reach out for My understanding and wisdom. Resort not to blind decisions. Reach out to Me for My direction in all things. Be sensitive to the nudging of My Spirit. Run not in circles.

[Father, what is the difference between intensity and being tense and overanxious?] Intensity is pressing in, knowing that I will bring to pass that which you are contending for, that I will bring to pass that which you are pressing in for. Being over anxious and being tense is synonymous with doubt. It is trying to twist My arm by doing all the right things to get Me to bring it about. Be not tense. Be not over anxious, but stand still, intently still, with perseverance of spirit, with rejoicing and thanksgiving, stopping the enemy at every turn, allowing no infractions; and see the salvation of your Lord. I am fighting for you, and ours is the victory.

Continue to stand tall in My Spirit. Maintain an intense, alert spirit. Draw on My wisdom and discernment. This has been a learning period. Hold on to what you have gained through the experience. Intensity is freedom. Straying in either direction toward tenseness or letting down in the spirit is being bound. Stay free!

Be determined and confident in Me. Set your shoes straight in the pathway of life. Have I not said, "Turn ye not to the left nor the right?" Even though it may seem logical and right to make an abrupt deviation from the path, never make that deviation, no matter who clamors for it, or how logical it may seem, or how reliable the source, without first checking with Me.

Hold on to the truth that I have given you in your walk with Me. Maintain a wary watchful eye for deception. Maintain a diligent eye, and walk in My Spirit night and day. Cease not your search for truth and a closer walk with Me, for I am the rewarder of those who diligently seek Me and long to know and understand My precepts. Maintain your intensity, and walk straight and tall in My Presence, in My Spirit.

Stand forth strong in My Word, for My Word has made you strong. Continue to feed on My Word with a fervor, for it is My will for you to know My Word, to digest My Word and to understand My Word. Many through the ages have read My Word, but few have come to Me to understand My Word as I understand it. Continue to come to Me for understanding as you read and digest My Word. Many rewards lie therein. Be diligent, and rejoice as I feed you and strengthen you and sustain you through My Word. Rejoice and continue on, My child, for nothing can derail your course, for I have set your course, and it is a sure course leading to life.

Walk boldly as a lion, for I am your mane to bring you strength and success. Wear that mane proudly and with confidence. Stand tall in My Spirit, for I stand tall with you and in you. Do not withdraw, but advance with shouts of joy, for ours is the victory, now and forevermore.

Faith that is firm is also patient! Have I not spoken of patience before? Let patience have its way in your life and in the lives of those around you. Let faith stand tall in your heart, statuesque and immovable, for have I not planned and shall I not carry out to the nth degree. Lift those up to Me whom I give to you with perfect trust and a patient heart, for I shall move upon them, I shall perform all that I have decreed, but none of it can you bring to pass. Only I can bring to pass all that I have decreed. So stand firm, stand fast, stand tall, with assurance that My will shall come to pass in My time, not thine. Frantic hurriedness brings mistakes and failure. Patient plodding brings My victory and My success. Be that patient plodder in My Kingdom, for together we shall win!

Prizes in the natural are won by sacrifice, determination and endurance. Prizes in the spiritual realm are won in the same way, that of sacrifice, determination and endurance. Be faithful to your high calling, and you shall be the recipient of prizes beyond estimation. Continue on! Continue on! Let not up in your quest of wisdom, discernment, perception and a Walk with Me. They are and shall all be yours; for those who ask, receive; and those who seek, find; and to those who knock at the door of the Kingdom of God, the door shall be opened; and they shall walk in with joy. Continue your quest, for your reward is sure.

Rest in My love. Fear not the storms that gather, for just as surely as the clouds gather overhead, they will be blown away again, and the sun will shine brightly again and the storm will have left life giving rain to nourish My children in ways they know not of. Be refreshed each day, whether the sun shines or if the clouds are o'er head, for either way I bless you daily and bring forth My perfect will in your life and those I give you to love. I bless you My child, each day I bless you. My eye is upon you to bless you.

Worry not over your finances. Have I not provided in the past? So shall it be in the future. I do provide for My children in all things. I see the need even before they do and start making provisions for that need, that it might be met with perfect timing. Respond to that provision with joy. A way has been made. Step into My provision with assurance and peace. Leave all anxiety and frustration behind, and proceed with trust in My providing hand. It is I who am in charge: even in this. For do not My children need dependable and reliant transportation to take them to the destinations to which I lead them? The paths I lead you on shall be many and varied, but they shall be passable because I have provided for them. So strike out along the paths with confidence and assurance, for I do provide.

Lift your head high out of respect for Me in praise. Lift it high, for I shall sustain you and guide you. Be My armor bearer. An armor bearer is always prepared, loyal, reliable, true and dependable. He can always be depended upon at any time and at any cost. Handle each situation as it arises with confidence and assurance, for I shall not, I repeat, I shall not let you miss the mark. Each action shall be with precision, My precision. Act and react in perfect confidence in My guiding hand in your life. Peace and contentment are the watchwords this day, for are they not My gifts?

There shall be a way for each task that I lay before you. Through trust and perseverance, each task shall be completed well and in My time. Go forth renewed and refreshed in spirit and alive to My ways and leadings. Respond with alertness, trust, peace and joy. And so shall your days fall one upon the other as a patchwork quilt is sewn together to make a perfect whole, for each square is a whole unto itself and necessary to the whole. So, each day is a whole unto itself and necessary to the whole. And just as each square of the quilt is different, so will each day be different, but complete in every way. So rest in My love and protection and perfect will for you and yours, and rejoice as you see each day added to make you whole and complete.

Resist the enemy, and he shall flee from you seven ways. Walk straight and tall in My Spirit. Respond to those around you with open arms of acceptance and love. Relax in My Spirit. Refrain from much ado over nothing. Rely on Me in all things and all shall be as it should be. Be refreshed. Your report shall be pleasing to Me and to thee.

Draw, draw from the rivers of life that are flowing through you. As they flow out to others, you partake too. Rely on Me for every breath you take. Be more aware of My moment-by-moment Presence with you. Respond to My nudgings by having a quick and alert spirit attuned to My Spirit continually. My light shall shine ever brighter in you as your spirit becomes ever more attuned and aware of My Spirit in you and working through you. Let your light shine ever brighter.

I love you, My child. My love never wavers. My love knows no peaks or valleys. It is stable and never changing. That is why you can put your total trust in Me and never waver in that trust, just as I never waver in My love. Receive My love each day. Open your heart to it, and we shall rejoice together with each new day.

Chapter 14

Walk In My Peace

"And let the peace of God rule in your hearts."
Colossians 3:15a

Be at peace, My child. Just as trees have different seasons of growth, so must you. A tree may be surrounded by people or it may be isolated far in the forest, but neither has anything to do with its growth. As long as its Father is providing sunshine, water and nutrients, it grows in beauty and strength. It depends on the Father's care, not on outside stimulation or influences. So are you to be, the strong beautiful tree of My planting, nurtured by Me, drawing your source of life and growth from Me. Outside influences are nice and pleasant, but not necessary to that growth. There is a time for outside stimulation and sharing, and there is a time for quiet fellowship and communion with Me. Take the seasons as they come and rejoice in each. Respond to My love flowing out to you. Soak it up as a flower soaks up the rays of the sun. Without those quiet times of soaking up the rays of the sun, the flower becomes stunted. So the quiet seasons are necessary to the growth of My children, if they are to become solidly based. Otherwise they become flitterers, flittering from one thing to another and their growth is as the tall spindly stalk searching for the sun, instead of the strong solid stalk that has steadily soaked in the sun, soaked in My love. Rejoice in our quiet time together.

Express your needs and your views more clearly and precisely to Me. In this way can we more fully work together building trust and faith as we go. Do not be afraid of your negative feelings, for as you express them to Me, I can respond with the answer you need. Negatives held within remain negative and increase in their negative power. Negatives brought to the surface and expressed to Me can then be turned to positive and will continue to grow in its positiveness. So, anger expressed to Me can be turned from, "My anger at you God," to, "Thy Will be done." Negative to positive. So, do not hide your feelings from Me. Express them that they might be dealt with to your help and to My Glory.

Lay aside all disbelief and doubt, and stand tall in My Spirit. You say all is as it should be, so believe it for yourself. Take each day as it dawns as My gift to you, complete in every way. I am in control. Believe and continue to believe with constancy.

Lay aside your fears of failure, for we shall go on to victory. The victory is ours. Restored is your perseverance and determination to prevail in My Name, and succeed we shall. Proceed this day with the knowledge that I am with you to give you success.

You shall give forth simply and straightforwardly, that others might understand, just as My Word to you is simple and straightforward that you might understand. Lay before them the straight path of rejoicing into My Presence, into the inner court of My Presence. For I am with you to give you assurance and understanding of how to proceed. Rejoice this day and give thanks, for many shall respond and come forth with real thanksgiving and praise unto Me, and they shall know that their strength and salvation comes from Me. Now, go in peace

My child and be not afraid, but be at ease, for all shall proceed with ease in My Name.

Rejoice and be glad this day, for into your midst has come a light shining brightly and radiating, showing the way. Be not afraid, for I am with you to lead you every step of the way. Until now, you have not known the stamina of My Spirit. The groundwork has been laid, and My plans shall come to pass within your vision and experience. My peace is yours. My understanding is yours. My joy is yours, and My never-ending love is yours. Yours is the wealth of My Kingdom. Continue in your quest for My Word and My Ways.

Release unto Me your fears of repression, for I would not have you repressed but expressed as I have made you to be. Go forth filled with hope for the future, for My plans shall unfold as each day passes into its fulfillment. Use what you have and more will be given. Rejoice in the now. Use what you have to My Glory.

Prepare your heart to receive My goodness and prosperity. Prepare through vigilance, perseverance and dedication to My Word and My Presence. Carry forth My Word to you to prepare and rejoice, for the day draws near when My ways and preparations for you shall be seen.

Forbearance is a virtue. Don't try to change him overnight. Let your light shine in all its brilliance, and its radiance shall reach him. It shall! My light in you shall shine forth and warm him until his light from Me can take full hold to burst forth into brilliant light, and burst forth it shall. It only takes a spark to get a fire going. So, let the light in your heart continue to warm him, to bring forth the light within him. Warm him, don't burn him.

My child, rest in My love for you. Quit struggling, and
rest in My love. Recline with your heart at peace. Refrain from
struggling in the water. Float on My arms, instead. Do not let
up your stand of strength in My Spirit. One can float in
strength, but one cannot thrash from a point of strength.
Thrashing comes from weakness. Enjoy the view, the peace
and serenity.

Be at peace, My child. Do the flowers of the field struggle to receive the beauty of their raiment? No, they trust in the
Father's care and receive in due season. So shall it be with you.
Struggle not and be at peace, for in My time and at My command, each piece shall fall into place and come to pass as I
have set forth. Do not be ashamed nor disturbed by your lack
of "productive" activity. Even the beautiful flower of the field
must lie dormant in the field until spring. But then it rises to
new life and beauty. So be not perplexed nor puzzled by your
situation, but take each season as it comes, continually drawing
strength and taking each day as it dawns with joy and thanksgiving. For so shall it be that My Spirit shall be manifested in
ways that you know not of, and so shall you rejoice with Me as
it is revealed.

Lay before My feet your desires and your plans. Let Me
make the plans and lead the way, for My ways are higher than
your ways, and My plans come forth with rejoicing and much
fruit. Be not afraid to express your desires to Me, but once they
are expressed, leave them with Me. You will rejoice to see how
I bring just the right things to pass. So bring forth your desires
and lay them on the altar, and go your way in peace.

Remove sin and remain in My love. The Words of My
Spirit ring forth with clarity and truth. Cling to them with ever
increasing vigil, for they are strength to your bones and everlasting life to your soul. Fear not, My little one, but remain in

My love forever. Release unto Me your fears of rejection, of being forgotten. Paul was not forgotten during his years in the desert with Me. He strengthened and prepared, and I sent him out with Power and with My Word and with My Spirit. So shall it be with you. Strengthen! Become one with Me!

Raise your sails in praise to Me. Let My Spirit fill those sails and glide you ever so gently in the direction you should go. With gentleness and ease shall you traverse the way I have laid out for you, for your faith in Me has made your journey thus. Rejoice this day, and set forth your sails, that they might be filled with joy and song.

A place has been made for you, a place of safe haven and rest. And as you remain in that rest, I send forth My deliverance and rest upon those you love. The more at peace you are, the more at peace they will be. The more at rest you are, the more they will rest in Me and trust in Me. I am using you as a barometer. Remain in My love. Be at peace. Be at rest. Resist not the leading of My Spirit. Sail on!

I bless you child. Go your way in peace and serenity, and know that I am Lord of all situations. Let not your heart be troubled, neither let it be afraid, for I shall speak to you words of wisdom, and you shall know from whence cometh the source of your strength. It cometh from a glad heart. Your ways have been laid out on a straight and narrow path. Abide in My peace. Abide in My love. Rely on My steadfast love. Reach forth your hand and receive from Me strength and resourcefulness. Go forth with singing and a glad heart.

Inner beauty is brought forth through pressure, to teach one to respond to pressure with peace. It is a process that must be lived step-by-step. Rejoice in the becoming. My blessings are upon you My child.

Listen, My child, with earnestness. I shall remove from you all sense of guilt and reparation, that you might go forward in My strength and not your own. Continue on with steadfastness and sureness, for I shall be the bidding one to bring you success. Sureness and steadfastness shall come to you with alacrity. Be at peace, My child. Calm your inner being, and be released from tension and inner stress.

Today shall stand on its own, a day of joy and gladness, for again I shall be the bidding one. I shall lead you with great love and compassion and with a continual hope and glory radiating from your heart. Relax My child. Relax and know My will for you, to have a loving and pure heart.

Rest, rest My child. Be at rest in My Presence this day. There are many days for running and doing, but this is a day for rest and contemplation. Refresh your spirit through communion with Me. You shall see that all things work together for good to those who love Me. So hasten not to accomplish much this day in the physical realm. Accomplish much in the spirit realm with Me. Stretch forth your wings. Extend you tent walls of understanding in My Spirit. Blessed shall our time together be. Eternal progress shall be made of a magnitude you know not of. So spread your wings with thanksgiving and song, and I shall make of your ways an oasis in the desert. You shall know more of Me and I shall dwell more with you. Haste makes waste. Dwell this day with Me at My pace. Our relationship shall grow day-by-day as you seek to know Me in such a way, for I do reward those who diligently seek Me.

Chapter 15

Stand Tall In My Love

*"According as He hath chosen us in Him
before the foundation of the world,
that we should be holy and without blame before Him in love."*
Ephesians 1:4

Ours is a relationship of love, one of mutual respect, for you have known Me in a way that few have grasped. You have seen My hand performing wonders and blessings for you and your loved ones. You have traversed the way with Me, seeking My guidance at every turn and blessing My Name. My child, My love flows out to you strongly. There is no area in your life that My love cannot touch and re-create. Stay close to that love. Draw on that love. Depend on that love. And as you do this, that same love flows from you to others. That drawing and dependence on My love creates a flow of My love from Me to you to others: a flow that is continuous. So continue to draw and depend on My love, that others in need might receive My love through the flow of My love through you. They must become receivers before they can become transformers. Beauty and strength come through My love. All gifts of My Spirit are created through My love. So are your gifts to be, created through My pure love given forth. Stand firm, stand tall in My love, for you are My beloved child in whom I am well pleased.

Life is like a maze. You can find your own way by continual running into solid walls that lead nowhere, and then backtrack and start over again; for there is only one way, My way; or you can let Me guide you through the maze every step of the way. The end of the way is life with Me. Some through obstinate self-will never find the conclusion I have for them. They refuse My help, depend on themselves and never make it. Depending on Me contains the promise of success and victory. The more one depends on My guidance the fewer dead ends one encounters. Total dependence on Me and faith in My guiding hand insures a smooth, safe path to life and victory. Continue on as you have. Continue on, as you have. Blessed is the one that comes in the Name of the Lord.

Glory in the Highest! Peace on earth, good will toward all who love Me! Fire shall consume and burn away the dross, and all shall be clean and pure before Me. Worry not, little one, for My promises shall come to pass in ever-increasing numbers, and your heart shall sing, and your spirit shall rejoice. Glory and honor, peace and joy belong to those who practice and obey My Word. I do bless My little flock with blessings too wonderful for words. It is My great pleasure to bestow upon them the Kingdom, My Kingdom. So, go forth with a singing heart full of rejoicing and love. Pour forth that love on your loved ones, as I pour it forth on you.

I set before you a blessing and a curse, as I do before all of My people. Serve Me with gladness of heart, and lean not unto your own understanding. Stand upright in spirit, with no guile therein. Prepare within your heart a garden of praise and thanksgiving, and know without a shadow of a doubt that I am with you. My rod and My staff do comfort you and guide you to green pastures and beside still waters, and do refresh you and uphold you. Hasten not to strive for greatness and pleasures. False striving brings forth the curse, which is loss of communion with Me. Never let this happen. Continue on with thanksgiving and song. Let Me clear the way and set the pace. Do not get ahead of My guiding hand, for I shall guide you with sureness in the way that you should go. So be at peace within your heart. Take each day as I bring it unto you, with a song in your heart and praise upon your lips. Let it be as I have said, for upon thee and thine, I shall pour out the riches of heaven and the blessings of My heart.

You shall not make a mistake but shall know that to which I lead you. The signs shall be clear to lead the way. You shall see clearly. Your way is clearly marked and nothing can detain you. Sufficient to you is each day. Wonder not, nor let your heart be puzzled. You shall know. You shall know. Be patient, for soon all shall be revealed. Hasten not. Hasten not, but rejoice and take each day as it comes, with thanksgiving and song.

March forth unafraid, undaunted, for My will for you is sure. It is vouchsafed, for has it not been set forth from the foundation of the world. My will shall come forth as I have proclaimed. *Yours is to be, Mine is to do!* Rest, My child. Rest in My love. Let the sands pour forth in their time unhindered. Be at peace, and each sand shall bring forth the required result.

Stand still and know that I am God. I shall guide you and protect you forever. The soles of your feet shall be refreshed as you walk on dry ground, safe from the raging waters, safe from the tempest round about, safe and secure from all alarm. For nothing shall harm you, My child. Stay close to My heart. Rest in My arms and reserve your best for Me. See if I do not reserve My best for you. Turn not aside from your first love, and partake of the abundance that I provide for My beloved. So arise, shine and be fortified by My love and provision for you, for I shall guide you by My hand, and love you forevermore.

Arise, shine, let your light shine, for I have brought you out of the darkness and into My brilliant light. The works of your hand shall prosper, and you shall be delighted to know of My plans for you. Be not ashamed of your days of darkness, but know that through them has come the brilliant light that you now see. So rise up in strength and joy and partake of the newness of life coming in you. Rejoice, for My strength has become your strength, and My joy has become your joy. My peace has become your peace, and My patience has become your patience, and My endurance has become your endurance. The desires of your heart have come to pass for all to see and rejoice in with you. So sing Hallelujah, sing Hosannas and sing with great abandon, for we have walked the highways and the byways together, and you have come up strong with wisdom and understanding. Continue on with complete abandonment of your will to Mine, for we shall continue to progress together with success and with jubilation.

Shout for joy this day, for into your hands have I put everlasting peace and joy. At your request, I have thus purged your heart from animosity and fear. You now know the source of that everlasting peace and joy and how to maintain it at all cost. So relax and be at ease, for your heart shall respond with gladness at every turn in the road, and your spirit shall rejoice with Me at every new piece added to your life.

The time has come to prepare a way of service. Continue strengthening and rejuvenating and recharging. The task is at hand and you shall be amazed at the strength of My hand in your life and those you love. Resist the enemy, and he shall flee from you seven ways. Hold onto My hand and continue along the road with Me with joy and gladness of heart.

My Words ring loud and true. You shall know them, receive them and obey them. Tarry not in indecision. Step forth boldly in and on My Word. My Word to you is clear, precise and trustworthy. Go forth in safety and sureness. My Word shall not fail you but shall sustain you all the days of your life, and you shall dwell in the House of the Lord forever.

Muster your strength this day and proceed with diligence and determination to set your house in order. Deliver a receipt of work well done. Proceed with lightness of heart, and I will lighten your load as you go, and make it seem light. One step at a time brings success. Go forth with diligence and song. Sing forth praises, and let your heart sing.

Get off your high horse and love. Let love be your aim in all things. Relieve your tension through love. Show forth love in little ways, ways of thoughtfulness and cheer. Leave not undone today what you can do tomorrow. Show forth your love by doing it today. Blow not your own horn. Let it go unheralded and unnoticed. Do it for Me in love for them. Relieve your anxiety through diligent loving. Relieve your self-contempt through aggressive releasing of your burdens and rejections and disappointments and disunities unto Me. Let Me carry them. Don't hold any of them to yourself. Drop them into My arms in an eternity of forgetfulness. Live only in the joy of this moment with Me, with My love. For what is past is past, totally past, and what is in the future is in the future beyond your reach. All you have is the loving, peaceful and pure present, if you allow it to be. What others think of you does not matter. It is what you think of them that matters, if you have given all over to Me and love them with a pure undefiled love. So release unto Me all the garbage, and begin to love with a pure love undefiled by past feelings. Such love brings peace and release from tension. Release from tension shall come to you as you feed on My Word and fly as a new eaglet into the clear blue sky of My truth. Try it, you truly will like it. Sincerity comes from a pure undefiled heart, from which all contamination has been released unto Me. So go forth this day, resting in the assurance of My love, free to bestow that same love upon others, unrestricted by the past or the future.

Go forth this day under My protection and under My leadership. No ill shall befall you, and all shall be under My grace. Let not your heart be troubled, neither let it be afraid, for into your hands has been given the everlasting gift of peace, the peace that I give that nothing can shake nor disturb. Let the stones fall where they may, but nothing can disturb that inner trusting and peace that I, your Lord, have bestowed upon you. Peace, be still. Your peace shall extend to others and be as the Balm of Gilead. Be that restorer of My peace. Be a peacemaker, for you are My creation, lacking in nothing, for all that I have is yours. So go forth this day with assurance of My guiding hand as moved by My loving heart. Draw forth My love. Give forth My love, and lean not unto your own understanding. Give forth! Give forth! My peace is with you, My child, to be My channel of blessing. Go forth this day with anticipation of observing My handiwork in your life and in the lives of others. Rejoice and sing for joy.

Lay aside all burdens, grief and guilt. Let Me fashion for you a protective raiment of purest gold. It shall protect you forevermore against yourself. Let not your heart be troubled, neither let it be afraid. Let it ride on the wings of My Spirit, free from frets and worries, free from tension and strife. For unto you this day have I given riches untold, abundance of fortitude against storms, resilience against turmoil, and armor against tension. Listen, My child, as I tell you of things to come. There shall come into your life a joy too great for words. The works of your hands shall prosper, and you shall know of My mighty power in your life, to seek and to save. Let it never be said in your house that the Lord your God is not a Great God, for mightily have I moved in your life, and in your loved one's lives. Joy too great for words shall come upon you and raise you up. So, come into My Presence with thanksgiving and praise and a willing heart and spirit, ready to do My will, for unto you have I given irrefutable gifts, unfathomable joy and indisputable wisdom. Enter into My courts this day with praise and worship, and place your hand in Mine, and we shall walk together this day in unity and transcending peace and joy. Lift up your heart and rejoice. Fortitude brings joy, for it brings patience, endurance and trust, trust in Me. Rest in that trust. For unto you this day have I given the desires of your heart. A heart full of love, forever loosed from fear and strife, released from tension, and free to soar in perfect peace and joy, in constant unity with My Spirit. Unto you have I bestowed these gifts, that you might be a channel of blessing to others. Stray not out from underneath My protective covering. Lift up your heart to Mine. My strength is your strength. Draw from Me as you have need of My attributes, for all that I have is yours. Think on this and rejoice. Hallelujah! The Heavens ring forth with joy! Rejoice this day and go forth with a merry heart!

You are blessed, My child. I have put upon you the way to liberty and freedom. No longer shall the whims and desires of the flesh overwhelm and prevail, but by My Spirit, saith the Lord, shall you be motivated. Tie a string of remembrance upon your heart forever, that you might remain in that freedom forevermore. Relinquish not that freedom at any cost. Let Me feed you beside still waters. Let Me bring you into green pastures of serenity and peace and love resplendent in all that you need.

Chapter 16

Listen To Your Heart

"Behold, I stand at the door, and knock:
if any man hear My voice, and open the door,
I will come in to him, and will sup with him, and he with Me."
Revelation 3:20

Let your heart guide you, for I shall guide you step-by-step, and you need to know the leading of your heart and not your mind from moment-to-moment. My guidance is available to you moment-by-moment, if you listen to your heart, for am I not residing in your heart to bring you peace, joy, understanding and guidance? Listen to your heart, for it is I speaking. Let not your mind be heard, but your heart.

Store up. Feed on My Word. Let it be sustenance to your body and your spirit. The ways of My Spirit are varied and many. You are learning of My heart word to you. Let My wisdom carry you through, through heart leading. You shall know. You shall know, and we shall fellowship together as you learn to follow My heart leading. Listen carefully, continually.

My child, listen to the leading of your heart. Lean not unto your own understanding. Let not your heart be troubled, neither let it be afraid, for I have your comings and your goings all recorded in My Book, and it shall all come to pass with ne'er a thread out of place. All shall be born out in My time and at My leading. Let not your weariness be a stumbling block to you, for in your weakness I am strong in you. Tarry not in doubt over this, but let Me have My way in this, too, for your weakness shall give way to strength as the darkness of the night gives way to the brilliant rays of dawn. Be refreshed in this knowledge, and go your way, taking each moment as it comes with rejoicing and song. There is time enough for much activity; now is the time of quiet in My Presence. Cherish this time together, for it is like none other, and you shall relish it in days to come. Relax in My Presence, and lift up your heart to Me with steadfast love and adoration. Let Me be your place of habitation, just as you are Mine. I am your steadfast rock of protection. There is a cleft in that rock for you. Nestle into that cleft with all trust and love, as a child snuggles into its parents lap for warmth and affirmation. I long to be that quiet place of rest and affirmation for you. Have I not prepared a place for you? Enter in and partake of all that I have provided for you. The door is open and all has been prepared for you. Rest in Me, child. Rest in Me. One step at a time. When you have rested and learned of that quietness in Me, then we can proudly step out together in service and in love. Learn of My love for you, child. Rely on and perceive in deeper levels of that love. It is yours. Receive! Receive! Receive! Receive, and then become a restorer, an instrument of restoring that love to the brethren. It is yours, My child. Reach out and receive it.

I stretch out My hand to you, My child. Stretch out your hand to Me and grasp it with the firm, trusting grip of a child. Stand forth in honor and in truth, with fortitude, for ours has been the victory and ours shall be the victory. This day you shall see a glimmer of that victory that I have for you. Let your light shine. Hold it not back, but let it shine and warm others with its radiance, and it will come back to you and warm you. Be not afraid. Let not the times disturb you. They shall not harm you. Go your way in peace. Know My peace that passeth all understanding, and rest on My Word to you.

Go forth this day with a smile on your face and a song in your heart. Many shall know of your joy as you walk with Me and follow My leadings to you. A way has been made into that complete joy. It is yours. Radiate that joy within your heart. My hand is upon you to bless you this day.

Break away from all restraints upon your spirit, restraints of faintheartedness. Strike forth with fortitude and purposefulness. Break away from traditions of men that bind. Be set free from fetters of traditional views that bind. Seek out My truth each day, and move on that truth. Leave behind old ways that have always led to dead ends, that have never led to Me and My Presence. Be a watchman on the wall and carry My truth within you as a prized historian carries truth within him. For it shall be My truth, unpolluted by years and years of men's tradition. Search for My truth with renewed vigor and stamina. Revel in that truth with renewed and newly awakened perseverance. My Spirit shall lead you in your quest for truth, and you shall know as you walk which is and which is not from My Word. Practice My Presence with ever increasing determination and joy in receiving from Me: My truth, My Word, and the fulfillment of My Love.

Release your own spirit to hear My Word more clearly, for I long to share with you more of My Kingdom here on earth and in Heaven. Worry not as to others hearing My voice. Stick to basics. You hear My voice! Do not try to extract the twig from another eye. Tend to the log in your own and I will tend to the twig in your friend's eye. Now you have the idea. Judging, even in the wrappings of love and concern is still judging, and ties My hands to work in their lives and yours. Once again, when you see a problem in another's life unrecognized by them, lift it up to Me and leave it there. Don't take the problem upon your own shoulders. It was never meant to rest there. It will weigh you down and block both of your progress in Me. That is why I say, "Release them unto Me." Take not the burden to yourself.

The sacrifice of love is given and shown by one who restrains himself from over-indulgence and greed. Restraint comes about as a result of love and gratitude toward Me, My Spirit and My blessings. Gluttony, greed and ungratefulness are one. See that you put them to flight at every turn and avoid them like the plague. Unto you shall I give the keys to right living, as you rely on My strength to lead you and sustain you day-by-day. Follow the straight and narrow road that leads to life, and leave the side roads to others who will not follow My leading. Continue on with fresh resolve to do My bidding and follow My leading. New horizons and vistas shall open up to you, as you proceed with a determined heart and a spirit filled with My love and joy.

Set your tent pegs out a little farther. Enlarge your tent's capacity for Me even more, that I might be an even greater part of your life, consecrated and restored unto Me. Blessed is the one that cometh in the name of the Lord. Blessed is the one who trusts in the Lord for all things: wisdom, strength and sustaining love. His way shall be made an oasis in the desert and a life of everlasting joy and peace. Let your light shine forth and your feet walk the highways and the byways with an ever increasing awareness of My Presence with you. You shall know more and more of the magnitude of My love for you and of My unending purpose of joy in your life and in the lives of your loved ones. So open up your heart even fuller to receive Me and My Spirit, for there are vistas not yet seen up ahead that shall make your heart sing and shall bring praise to My Name.

Your face shall shine as the noonday sun, and your heart shall be merry and sing with praises. With delight shall you draw from the well of My blessings for you, and you shall know from whence cometh the saying, "Arise, shine, for unto thee have I given the keys to My Kingdom." My heart delights in you and takes pleasure as you delight in Me.

The fresh dew, the rejuvenating, life-giving dew of My Spirit, sparkles like diamonds on My beloved ones, and they go forth refreshed and rejoicing with each new day. Sing a new song unto Me, filled with joy and anticipation of each new day that I have planned for thee and thine. My heart sings, too, with joy for you, and the trees and the birds and flowers sing with anticipation of spring. Yea, the winter is past, and the time of spring is upon us, the time of rejuvenation, joy and singing, a time of newness. Burst forth this day with the anticipation of the newness of spring, and let your heart sing and rejoice. Be My songbird, and sing a new song of spring.

Stretch forth your wings and fly, My songbird. Let your voice twittle with the song of love coming from your heart. Break forth in song, as I lead you through the day, and let your heart sing unto Me with joy and alacrity. Your wings shall not be clipped. You shall see, for My blessing shall be upon you, and we shall sing together to My Glory and Honor. Go forth from this day with diligence of character and fortitude of spirit and righteousness, My righteousness, within your heart.

My servant you shall be, and My watchword to you shall be and is, "rejoice, rejoice, rejoice," for unto you have I given the Keys to My Kingdom which are faith, patience, fortitude and reliance. Lift up your heart and rejoice this day, for I see before you a never ending road of hope and peace, kept alive by faith.

Your heart shall be the resting place for many that I shall send your way, for your heart has come into My peace and knows the way for others searching to find the way to that peace, My peace. Be that peaceful way station for them along their arduous way, for they shall find rest and peace for their souls; a rest and peace that only I can give to them. *Be, and I shall do!*

Your feet shall walk the highways and the byways shod with the message of peace, My peace; the peace I give to all who would but receive. You are blessed, for you have received My peace, and now you are to go forth, bearing the good news of My peace to all peoples. Step forth with vastitude, for My hand is upon you to bring you success and to lead you with sureness and wisdom. Go forth, then. This day shall bring you fullness of joy, as you walk by My side and at My leading.

Let Not Your Heart Be Troubled

"Let not your heart be troubled; ye believe in God, believe also in Me."
John 14:1

My child, listen to Me with your ears wide open, for I have much to teach you, much to share with you, and the time is short. Let Me imprint upon your heart the wisdom of the ages, wisdom from above, wisdom from My heart to your heart. Straight is the path and narrow is the way. March down that path with singleness of heart and mind. My Spirit in you brings forth much fruit for your future growth. My Spirit in you rejoices as we go from Glory-to-Glory, as each new day brings forth new warfare and new victories. March forth victorious! March forth undaunted! March forth with joy!

Lift up your heart and sing this day, for unto you have I given joy, great joy, an everlasting joy of peace and tranquility, peace of mind and spirit. Enter in this day into the blessings that I have reserved for you. Let the peace and joy that I have given you sing forth from your heart this day. The gift is yours, My child, to give forth from a heart filled with praise and thanksgiving. Lavish My gift of peace and joy upon those who hear, as you sing from the heart. Be a restorer of My peace and joy, through song. Sing forth My blessings upon the people. Go forth with the assurance of My hand upon you and My love surrounding you in all that you do. Break forth, in joyful song!

My ways come as small thoughts in the back of the mind, sometimes accepted, sometimes unaccepted. If unaccepted by those who love Me, I bring the desire into their hearts, step-by-step, until that desire is as My desire. If accepted, I strengthen that acceptance, step-by-step, until it is the joy of their heart to do My will. Ponder and worry not as to the consequences. Let Me work a work in your heart, according to My perfect will. I never leave My children dangling without a purpose. Let Me bring peace to your heart, a peace that cannot be shaken, a peace that says, "I know that I know that I know that this is God's will for me."

Lay before Me all anxieties and worries, for have I not planned, and shall I not carry forth that plan to completion? Nothing shall be left wanting in between. My hand shall cover all the bases. Be of good faith and steady trust, for all is in My hand and under My control, and nothing shall go astray. You shall be well pleased. Go forth this day with renewed assurance and peace in your heart.

Mount up as on eagles' wings and soar, and glide with freedom through the vastness of My Kingdom with Me. Taste of the richness and vastness that My Kingdom provides for those who love Me and revere Me. My Kingdom is unlimited and unfathomable. Let Me bridge the gap between your understanding, which is meager, and My wisdom, which is limitless.

Go forth unafraid and rejoicing, for though the winds blow and the waves rise up, I shall stay their hand against you. My peace and protection is ever present and with you. Back not off, but stand your ground, and go forward with assurance and decisiveness. Nothing shall thwart you or overcome you, so press on with steadfastness. I shall guide you. I shall lead you, and all shall be well. I shall be the bit in your mouth. Fear not.

Start out one step at a time. Start out slowly. Let your peace and joy be evidence of your sincerity. Be at peace. Be at rest. Be My vessel for peace. Bring peace where there is turmoil. Be My healing balm. Let not your heart be troubled, neither let it be afraid, for into your midst I shall send My assurance, My love and My unmerited grace. You be; I'll do! Reach out your hand in peace, bringing My assurance. Carry My banner of peace and love, and I shall do the rest.

Stretch forth your wings this day in anticipation of things to come. Mighty is My hand upon thee and thine, to bring forth much fruit. Mighty are the deeds that you shall perform at My hand and at My leading. Let not up your intensity for the days of preparation draw to a close and the days of fruition come nigh. Reach out your hand and heart to Me in total trust and reliance. Say unto your heart, "Mighty are the deeds and ways of My Lord. I will trust Him forever." Go forth this day in total trust. I am with you and you shall see order and peace come from confusion. Rely on Me to bring it about. My ways shall prevail, and they who know Me shall know My peace.

The Great Writings show forth My mercy and continual care and protection to those who look to Me and follow My ways. Blessed are they who look to Me with love and trust. The watchwords are peace and assurance. They are My gifts. Receive them daily. Never let go of their blessing over you. Stay within their covering. Let your heart rest within their folds. My peace and assurance I give unto you, not as the world gives peace and assurance, unpredictable and with guile, but My perfect peace I give unto you, immovable, impenetrable and irrevocable. BE at peace. BE at rest. BE in My Presence continually.

Stretch forth your hand and heart to Me, and receive from Me the wisdom you need. It is yours to receive. Your days are all recorded in My Book of Life. Each day shall bring forth that which is necessary to the whole. Reflect back and see that this is so. Restoration it shall be for thee and thine. My time of restoration is here, and many shall rejoice that have waited with expectancy. Patience, rewarded. Surefootedness is brought forth through sustained patience. Surefooted you shall be.

Lay hold of serenity, for serenity shall be the byword, and be a peaceful retreat from the rigors of battle. That peace, once attained, shall never depart. Coming into My peace looses your loved ones, frees them to come into My peace, themselves. First, they are receivers of My peace and love through you, but eventually, they, too, become transformers and transmitters of My peace and love. Be at peace, My child. Let that peace pervade your home and your loved ones. Let Me continue to make of your heart and your home a haven of My peace and of My love.

Listen, My child, with a compliant and humble heart. Turn not to your own understanding. Turn constantly to Me for My understanding and wisdom. I shall not let you down or forsake you. Nestle in close, and rely on My constant care. Lighten your load still further. Go forth unencumbered by your own expectations of yourself and those around you. Loose your heart to respond in Me, to let My responses come forth unencumbered by your self image. Release unto Me your plans and expectations and let Me bring forth into perfection your time allotted. My peace reins within your heart and shall be the motivating power to bring forth My will in your life and in the lives of those you love. Be not anxious, and worry not, for My plans shall prevail, and My will shall come forth. Be at peace.

Let not your heart be troubled. Let not your mind devise plans that I am not in. Let Me form each day from nothing. Let Me be the Master Mind. Choose whom you will serve and follow. Choose My perfect plan as it unfolds or choose deviations devised by you. It is so simple when left to Me and so complicated when the human mind takes over. Open your heart to your Savior, and let Me bring forth unto perfection each moment, each day. You shall see. You shall see and be pleased.

Thunder and lightning herald the approach of a storm. Many times, I have loosed unto you the desires of your heart, but you have heard the thunder, and you have seen the lightning and the gathering clouds as you have pressed forward for the fulfillment to be seen. Press forward now. Let not your heart sink at the gathering of the clouds, for in My mind's eye, I see the fulfillment, not as if from afar, but as if it were on the threshold of your heart, for there it is.

My ways are imperceptible to those floating on the sidelines, but many times I have shown you the beauty of My Kingdom, and you have been delighted. Now, I shall show you what it means to be My disciple, steadfast, immovable and unafraid. You shall see more than you have seen in a lifetime, and you shall remain unruffled in the shadow of My wing, for My pinions shall protect you, uphold you and show you the way. Many shall be the upheavals, but nothing shall cause you defeat. Resting in the power of your Maker and friend shall bring you through, and you shall know the sweet savor of victory. Defeat shall be unknown to you, for I have made of you a strong and sturdy warrior in My Kingdom. Your feet are shod with granite, and your heart is warmed by My love. Your buckler and your shield have I woven together with your praise and thanksgiving. So, stand up and be counted in My army. Go forth with My banner waving in the breeze, and I shall make of you my servant, one in whom I am well pleased, and I shall send you forth with pride, and we shall prevail!

Fasting and prayer this day shall release your spirit into My way for you. It shall place you once more in the pathway of peace and tranquility that your loved ones may once again bask in the warmth and life-giving flow of that peace and tranquility. They have experienced a disruption in the flow and shall be aware of its regained flow to them. Step out reluctantly this week. Let Me feed you with rivers of living water, of life-giving nourishment. Then, we shall step out together with regained strength and fortitude.

Stay close to My Word this day. Let your heart be like a sponge soaking in My Word to you this day. It shall be a day of growth and a day of stabilizing. Bring forth your desires to Me, and we shall discuss them. Press forward with the assurance of My guiding hand. Go forward. Move onward, but stick close to My heart.

Standing in the gap is not always easy, but a necessary part of a walk with Me. My pinions are outstretched to hold you up, so never fear, but go forth with fortitude of spirit, knowing My Word to you with assurance and praise upon your lips. Your days shall be filled with My anointing, and your nights shall be lifted up to Me in praise. You shall be a watchman upon the wall, bringing forth unto Me labors of love. Go forth with singing and with praise and know My love for you is boundless and shall bring forth fruit. Your body shall know from whence cometh the saying, "Rise and be healed in the Name of Jesus," and it shall respond with alacrity, for unto you this day have I given the desires of your heart. Let not your heart be troubled, but know of My deliverance for thee and thine.

Chapter 18

Stand Tall In My Spirit

*"By whom also we have access by faith into this grace
wherein we stand, and rejoice in hope of the glory of God."*
Romans 5:2

Come to Me with love and peace in your heart. Open unto Me the desires of your heart, your frustrations, your weaknesses and your blessings and causes for rejoicing. Let Me share each and every response that you experience, be it positive or negative.

Together, we shall sow seeds of peace where there is only frustration and seeds of love and concern to the cut off ones, the isolated and the brokenhearted. Your way is lightened and brightened by Me. Each step that you take is sure and secure. Go forth with singing and song, and let your heart rejoice and be glad.

Time shall not be an obstacle. All shall fit in its appointed place at its appointed time. Restrain your heart from aggravation. Be at peace in your spirit, for My hand shall bring forth, and it shall be good, right and as I would have it. Stand tall in My Spirit, in assurance and faith in Me. My ways are safe and secure. They bring peace and joy to the trusting heart. Hold fast to the promises.

Remain steady, firm and steadfast, for I shall lead you in all things for your good and for the good of your loved ones. You shall prosper in ways you know not of, and you shall bless Me with a full heart to overflowing. Be still, and know that I am God every day. Come to Me with assurance and confidence. My will shall prevail.

Life radiates forth from My blessed ones, giving forth My life, My healing, and My blessing to those who would but receive. Give forth! I shall lead you to give forth, and My blessing shall go forth in abundance. Worry not as to the time or place, for My Spirit goes forth naturally to a receiving heart. Be a willing and open transmitter of My love, My life, My Spirit, My wholeness. You shall be amazed to see the results. Go forth with assurance of My love and grace to you. Rejoice and sing forth My praises.

Open up your heart to receive from Me wisdom, pure wisdom from Me. Loose yourself and your loved ones from the strong arm hold of the strong one. His strength shall not prevail over thee or thine, for My strength shall prevail. Loose yourself, now! Upon this house shall I build My Kingdom. My Kingdom shall prevail in each one. My authority shall come forth in each one, and each of you shall know of My leading wherein I speak, "Go here," and you shall go, and, "Go there," and you shall follow. Rejoice, for the night has passed, and the light of the new day dawns and is seen in brilliance.

This shall be a time of feasting at the watering hole. It shall be a time of drinking in My Spirit. Draw deeply, that your light may shine even brighter and release even more rays of My love and healing. Be refreshed, My child. Be refreshed in body, mind, soul and spirit. Life and honor, peace and joy, do I bestow on My loved ones. Rest in My love.

Stay close to My Word. Let not a day go by without pressing into My Word with all your heart. Let your way be mapped out each day as you study My road map. The roads will have less obstacles and be more passable. Study to make thyself a workman, approved in My sight.

Attune your heart to My Spirit in the days to come. Speak forth My Words with Spirit and with truth. With boldness let your way of grace be known, and proclaim that "Jesus is Lord to the Glory of God the Father." Stand straight and tall in My Spirit, and let your faith stand solid in Me. We shall go forth with joy abounding, and good works shall not be found lacking. My Spirit goes with you, to lead you and guide you. Store up My Word and My peace in your heart, and go forth with assurance.

It only takes a spark. So, do My people come forth. Be a spark spreader. Speak your words with assurance of My backing and preparation, both for you and for them. The groundwork shall be well laid, and together we shall see the fruit of our labors. Naught shall be in vain, for I see their needs and do provide and see to their resolution. Time shall tell, and you shall be pleased.

Don't allow yourself to be caught up in other peoples' problems. Once enmeshed, you become trapped along with them. Stay outside the problem, and lift them up to Me with all prayer and supplication, bringing them to Me with love and assurance of My hand of deliverance toward them. Release unto Me your anxieties and frustrations, and rest once again in My peace.

Stay close to My Word. It is life and breath to you. Ever increasingly have I brought you unto Myself through My Word. Feast on its magnitude and power to raise you up and give you strength. Your eyes shall see, and your ears shall hear, and your heart shall respond with ever increasing propensity and joy. Hang on to your perseverance and song. Let your heart sing.

My child, listen with all intentness. Forbearance is a virtue, yes, but along with forbearance must also be faith: faith that My hand outstretched will be able and willing to overcome all obstacles. Continue on, and let not up your vigilance, that My will might truly come to pass. Let your words be words of faith. Let your yeas be yeas and your nays be nays; and let your heart rejoice in peace, for My hand of deliverance is truly upon thee and thine, and My gift of peace is upon thee and thine. Your house is truly blessed, and that blessing shall spread even more to those who are added to it. Your tent pegs shall expand even farther, to include more that I shall send your way, and you shall be blessed. Open your heart to give forth of My Spirit. Open your heart to give forth of My love, and open your heart to give forth of My peace. Blessed is the one who comes in My Name. Their house shall be blessed forever. Remain in My Love!

My child, gather your strength around you, and don't let go. Let My Word to you be your strength and your shield and the battering ram against which nothing can penetrate. Surround yourself with My truth and My song to you. Sing and shout, for the day breaks forth, and you shall stand forth straight and tall and alert in My Spirit, in My army of believers who are the standard bearers. Lighten your way, through the peace of My Word to you. Bring forth abundant peace to those you touch, through the truth of My Word to you. Sing, for the night passes, and the new day dawns, bright, clear and radiant, through the peace, truth and strength of My Word to you. Race not into the new day, but take each new day as it dawns, letting each new day work its weight of gold in you.

Peace that passes all understanding is yours in Me. A lattice work of peace have I worked in your soul, that you will not be moved by the changing times or seasons, nor the wiles of men. Take heed that you seek refreshing of My peace to you each and every day. Proceed with caution, but proceed with diligence to do My will.

Days and nights shall become as one, as you seek to know My will for you. A river of life flows out from you, and many shall taste and be refreshed. Many shall know from whence cometh the saying, "Many are called, but few are chosen," for they shall see a call upon your life and the joy and peace that comes through responding. At times, you shall say, "I wonder," but in the next breath you shall say, "I know." Respond with clarity and with decisive action, that My truth may be made known and that My Spirit may be manifested with joy and with song. Sing, for the night is over. Sing, for the new day dawns. Sing, for the Sonshine blazes, with warmth and with joy and with love.

Let not your heart be weary in well doing, for unto you have I given My strength, My perseverance and My stamina, to uphold you in every circumstance. Your foot shall not stumble, your heart shall not be afraid, and your hand shall not weary in well doing in My Name. Your stamina shall be unto you an everlasting covenant with Me and shall prove to be an overcoming and formidable force. For nothing shall detain you, nor knock you from the ring, nor stay your hand for good, for we shall move out together as overcomers, as healers, as purchasers and redeemers, to bring forth My Word and My healing power to those who would but hear. Stand forth, strong in My Word, in My Spirit. Let your heart sing for joy. Sing out, with

radiance and joy, the blessings and righteousness of My Kingdom. I bless you, My child. Amen!

Rain on it now! Rain on your ways of responding to
tight situations. Respond with ease and praise in your heart,
and I will respond with graciousness to you. Open up your
heart to respond to My leadings with greater freedom of spirit.
I have spoken of My deep peace many times to you. It is to be
evident in all situations. My best work comes forth in tight situations. Allay your fears. React with a quiet and unperturbed
spirit, filled with trust and assurance. Many times shall you
have the chance to react unperturbed and at peace, at rest in
your spirit. Rain on doubt, unworthiness, restlessness, and indecisiveness. Run, don't walk. Skip, don't saunter. Pull down
the spirits of doubt and reluctance. Act now!

In My Father's House are truly many mansions, mansions fit for Kings. Have I not said many times, "Thou shalt
rule with Me." Your spirit is in preparation for that day. Each
day has its appointed measure. Each day has meaning for being. Until now, you have seen the limits imposed upon you.
Stretch forth your wings. The limitations are no longer there.
The bell sounds forth with joy, ringing forth statements of new
beginnings. Let your bell ring. Stand forth as a statement of
new beginnings. Leap forth into the new day!

Fasten your seat belt, and be prepared to move forward
with ever-increasing speed. Let not up your intensity for action, for My way for thee is being made known with ever increasing speed. Blessings and riches untold await thee and
shall loose thee to do My will with abandon. Action it shall be,
and My Spirit shall be manifested in all His Glory. Minute details shall fade into the background as the big picture becomes
more and more clear and distinct in the foreground. Sages of
old could not have planned this. They could not have seen the

magnitude of My plan for thee. So loosen your hold of the things that hold you down and get ready to fly. Position yourself to move with ease, unencumbered by tradition, or limits of the mind and soul. Fly we shall, with ease and grace. Sing, for the night is over. Sing, for the day has dawned. Sing, for the blessings abundant do come forth like the rising sun. Break forth! Break forth, with the assurance and radiance of My rising Son! Now unto thee, peace, joy and gladness of heart! Amen!

Chapter 19

Give Forth My Love

*"Seeing ye have purified your souls in obeying the truth
through the Spirit unto unfeigned love of the brethren,
see that ye love one another with a pure heart fervently."*
1 Peter 1:22

There is a time and a season for all things. Now is the time and the season for action. The time for quiet contemplation is over, and many shall profit from our time of peace and tranquility together. The Word shall reach those whose hearts are heavy with the load of fear, worry and doubt and whose spirits have not come to rest in Me. Their hearts shall rise up in the freedom and life of My Spirit. Lavish this, My gift of peace and life, which is love, upon these My children, and watch them grow in Me. Steady as you go, My child. Each piece of the puzzle shall fit firmly in place, and My will shall be made known to you, step-by-step. Strength of purpose shall be the driving force to lead you on, and I shall be with you every step of the way.

Warmth and affection are vital to growth in My Spirit. Be an example of the warmth and love that is Me. Be not sparing. There is always more than enough for each and every one, and you receive double what you give. Give without fear. Simply give. Giving lightens the load of receiving. My gift of love manifested in My children becomes magnified as they go forth sharing it, and bestowing it with ever increasing intensity and strength of purpose. Be a magnifier of My love to you. Give forth, as I give forth without reservation, without fear, without thought to oneself and how it is being accepted. Give forth without reservations.

My children cannot fail. If they believe in hurt and failure, it is theirs. If they believe in My love and protection, nothing can come nigh them but My love and My peace. They will never be put to shame. The trust of a child brings forth perfection. Nothing can alter the course of a trusting heart. Trust Me. Do not steel your heart to trust Me as one in a leaky boat in a raging stream. Trust Me as a carefree child being carried in your Father's arms. No course of action can derail you unless you allow it by agreeing to its power over you. There is no power greater than My power. Relax in My love for you.

Send forth blessings and words of wisdom each day. Feed My children as you have been fed, on a steady diet of My love and of My Word. My love and My Word are inseparable. One cannot fully be manifested without the other. Those who try, fail. Love, given without My Word, does not bring life. It is incomplete and brings frustration and pain. My Word, without My love brought forth, brings forth legalism, death and pain. It is a union of both My love and My Word that brings forth life, fulfillment, peace and My perfect joy. Be a restorer of My love, brought forth through My Word. Bring forth life in its fulness.

You have nestled in the warmth of My love for you, as shown forth by those you love. You have been bathed in the radiance of My love for you. Carry it forth into the cold and barren places that I shall carry you to. Pour forth the streams of My living love. There are two kinds of love: mechanical, natural love that lacks warmth and life, and My living love that brings healing and completeness to the receiver. Be a restorer of My living love. You have received. Now, give. Give forth with abundance. Give forth with no reservations. Give forth with exuberance. Give forth with quiet strength. Just give forth. Place your hand in Mine, and give forth as you draw forth from Me. When one is a transformer, one must stand totally at peace, giving forth My love, and the receiver, even though up-tight, will relax and begin drawing on that love and peace. Draw daily from the well of Living Waters.

Seasons follow one upon another. Seasons of refreshing have been ours, and now the doors are thrown wide open for you to enter into the ministry and give forth of My love to My children in need. You shall move with forthrightness, and your endeavors shall be met with joy and thanksgiving. You shall witness the infilling of My Spirit upon many who shall know of Me though your efforts of love. Redeem the time, for it is precious. Be a restorer of My love in many big ways and many small ways. My Spirit is upon you to move you in the way that you should go. Weary travelers along the way shall drink deeply of your Living Water. You have longed for this day. It is here. Stand tall in the power of My Spirit and give forth, that the richness of My Grace may be received in its fullness.

Prepare to step out with a deep reliance on Me. My hand shall steady you and lead you in the way you shall go. Be not afraid. I shall not let you waver, neither shall you be put to shame. Listen to My Word to you with renewed vigor and determination, and let us go forth together with joy and anticipation for the future. All things are in My hands, and you can rest assured of My love for you and My blessings upon you. Move forward with determination and strength, and let My Word to you show you the way.

Enter into the joy of your salvation this day. Be at peace in your heart. Let Me lead you step-by-step into what I have for you. Do not allow yourself to be pressured. Evidences of My love shall surround you, and you shall know each step to take along the way. My way for you is fastened securely in place and shall not miss the mark. Allow Me the freedom to work in your life and bring to pass those things that we both long for. Let not your heart be troubled. Stand ready and alert to move as I lead, but be not perturbed nor disturbed. Be at peace. Reign over your anxieties. Give them no room to grow. Be at peace. Let your heart sing. Blessed art thou, My beloved one. We shall walk together, step-by-step. Allay your fears and rejoice. Step out this day with a new freedom in your heart, a new trust in your spirit, knowing we shall prevail.

Teach your heart to listen with greater confidence. My Word to you is made known in many little ways. Prepare your heart to listen with ever-increasing adeptness. My Word to you is clear and straightforward. Meaningful words of love and guidance pour forth from Me to you. Let your heart be alert and ready, assured and at peace in the presence of My heart. Your ways are led by Me, and you shall not trip. Steady on, My child, with renewed confidence and vigor. Let your light shine with new radiance of My love. Singleness of mind and heart brings victory. Our days shall follow one upon the other with ever-increasing meaning and speed. Be prepared to move out, and be prepared to love and move in My love for you.

Sit in My Presence and be at peace. Be at peace this day. Let it be a day of blessed assurance. Let your heart sing with exuberance and joy. Lead the way this day in thanksgiving and praise. Loose your heart to rejoice, and those around you shall be loosed to rejoice. Sing Hosannas! Sing Hallelujahs! Sing Amens! Rejoice with abandon and with a merry heart! Enter in with joy this day. Let your joy be known. Kindle fires of thanksgiving and praise in the hearts of those you meet. Frowns shall become smiles, and sighs shall become laughs. Proceed with a light heart.

Ease on down the road. As each sand of the hour glass falls, so shall each step be taken, one-by-one. It is not the big blast but the continual pressing in that builds the strong foundation. Be not afraid of the slow start. Rest in My preparations and My love for you. Step-by-step, day-by-day, resolve to walk in what I have given you to walk in, and more will be added. Be not pressured nor grieved over lack of action. It is there. It is there. Remain in My peace for you. Do not let oppression knock on your door, for all shall go as I have planned. Remain unmoved by outside pressures. Simply move as I lead, step-by-step. Remain agile and alert. Be at peace, My child.

Worry not as to the whats or whys of the days to come. It is all in My hands, each day falling upon the other as I would have it. Each day shall be filled with joy and with My perfect peace. My will shall be made known to you, and each shall rejoice. Go forth with ever increasing joy and peace in your heart for the understanding shall be there, and your heart shall rejoice at the magnitude of My plans for you.

Speak My Word with all boldness, clarity and truth. Be not reticent. Let the joy and peace of My light shine brightly through you and about you. My Words shall pile up like treasures unto you, and you shall feed on them and be nourished and gain strength. Hasten not to bring forth. My Word to you is, "Patient plodding in a straight line with no side roads or detours." Patient plodding brings victory and success. Release unto Me your fears of failure. Freedom it shall be. Go forth in the knowledge and anticipation of our victory together. Straightforwardness shall bring forth much gain. My Word shall be manifest in many ways that you know not of. Rest in

My love for thee and thine. Let your light shine, and My light shall shine and radiate over all, to bring forth My victory and defeat over the enemy. Go forth in My light.

There are two factors, love and hate, with no in between, for lack of My total love is hate. Remain in My love, My child, and I shall love through you, and that love shall be a pure love, undefiled and unafraid. Many shall come to you to receive this My love, for it fulfills and brings completeness in Me. Rest in My love for you, and as you do rest in My love, it shall flow forth. Doubt not. Seek not to manufacture this, My love. Simply rest in My love and watch it flow out to these My children. My love shall flow out in any and all circumstances, unhindered by complacency and withdrawal. We shall go forth in joy, spreading My love liberally, with no restraints. Glory, Hallelujah! My love shall prevail!

Persevere

"If ye continue in My word, then are ye My disciples indeed."
John 8:31b

Brush yourself off, pick yourself up, and let's move on down the road ever closer together as one. Meaningful and full days lie ahead of us. Now is the time to prepare for them, that you be not sidetracked nor waylaid, for My will for you is strength and perseverance, ever moving forward in the power of My Spirit. Straightforwardness never ceases to be a virtue, and so shall you be. Enter into the fulness of My love for you. Repent of idleness of spirit and of heart. Be restored in every way. You are loosed into the fullness of My Spirit to walk and to move as I do lead in every thought, word and action. Watch each step fall into place as we do proceed together. Continue on! Continue on!

Wrestle not with your inadequacies. Simply say, "This I will do," and stick to it. Let it not be said that you had not the fortitude to persevere, for persevere you shall, and we shall see it through to the very end. Let your yeas be yea and your nays be nay. Strength of will shall see you through many a tight situation, and strength of will shall be yours as you do persevere with determination to be an overcomer in My Name.

Now that you have your feet back on the ground, you shall see each piece of the puzzle fit securely into place. Frustration is at an end, short-lived and dead. Your heart shall respond with My peace and your foot shall tread lightly, and yet solidly along the pathway I have laid out for you. Hasten not to conclude My dealings with you. Let each event be worked through to completion. Retreat not. Full steam ahead. Recoil not, but step forth with My assurance and faith in My guiding, leading hand. A way has been made that shall Glorify Me and please thee. Steady on, My child. Look not at the water, but look up, rejoicing in each step we shall take together. You are not alone, neither shall I forsake you nor abandon you. The footing is solid, though it seems slippery, and My hand shall steady you and not let you slip to have to start again. Rejoice, for the day of fulfillment is at hand. Go forth with a quiet, trusting heart.

Loose your mind from the circling, circling. You shall know what each day is to hold. Simply complete each task as I present it. Keep your focus on Me. With your focus firmly planted on Me, so that nothing or nobody can move you off that position, I am free to work in your life. You have moved your focus off of Me, onto the externals. Success cannot come in this fashion, only confusion, frustration and cobwebs and windmills, circling and circling of the mind. Heed well My words to you and get your focus back on Me and My way for you shall be clear and on track. Keep your focus steady on Me. We shall prevail together.

Ashes and rubble are the ways of man as brought about by arrogance and pride. See that your every act is prompted by Me and not by thee. Persevere in My Word, asking and receiving, instead of acting and then asking. Regard My Word and work, above all else. Set yourself to be My servant, blameless and upright. Steady yourself against Me through the purging of your body, soul and spirit, through the renewing of your mind through Me. Tarry not in indecisiveness, but move forward in faith and determination to do My will unflinchingly. I shall point the way with clarity and truth, and your heart shall rejoice and be glad.

Stand steady, My child. I have not left you nor forsaken you. Your house is still built on strong, sturdy rock and shall not be toppled. Look to Me to find your answer. Let My Spirit within be your guide. The outcome shall surprise you. Revert not back to old ways of responding with fear and frustration. I am still in the driver's seat, if you will but allow it. "Let go and let God." See Me as the engineer of your multi-faceted train of being. We shall not derail nor wander onto a wrong track. Our train shall arrive at its destination on time and intact. So be it!

Blessed assurance is yours, My child, this day. Out of the ash heap shall come answers to steady you and astound you. Tarry not in unbelief or doubt, but let your spirit be at ease in the security of My love for you. Place your hand in Mine, and walk step-by-step with Me this day.

Beware of intruders into your life: intruders of despondency, rejection and unbelief. Stand firm and tall. You are a full grown oak that cannot be toppled, unless you allow intruders to invade like termites. Your faith is strong and sure. Stand like the oak, both feet solidly planted and both arms outstretched in blessing and praise. I water and refresh the outstretched arms, and the oak, in turn, gives blessing and shade and refreshing to those who come within its outstretched boughs. Receiving and blessing. Receiving and blessing. The oak in its strength is a blessing to many. So shall you be.

Go forth this day with a merry heart dedicated to Me and striving to go forth unencumbered. A merry heart is as medicine. Carry forth My prescription, and see your body, soul and spirit come forth whole and well. Rise up and walk. Follow Me. Be healed in the Name of Jesus!

Peace that passes all understanding is yours My child. Cleave to Me and only Me. Let your light shine in the darkness and serve as a beacon light to those wandering in the darkness, who know not the light, which is Me. Perceive and discern as you walk in harmony with Me. Let not your heart be troubled, neither let it be afraid, but let it rest at peace in My perfect love for you. A softness has been given you to give forth of My blessings. Go forth. My shield protects you round about and My light shines about you, to show you the way. Let not your heart become disheartened at what you see. See, and seeing, believe!

Be watchful and alert this day to the resources that will come your way. Breakneck speed is not the answer, but a steady plodding down the path I have charted for you. Be at peace, and go forth this day with a song in your heart and blessings in your mouth.

Seated in the heavenly places art thou, ministered to by My angels. I meet every need as it arises and do not allow your foot to strike a stone. Strengthen your will to walk in My way. Weed out the thistles that are causing you discomfort and pain. Strengthen your resolve to walk totally in My will for you. Your faith shall make you whole. Believe, and it shall be. Go forth and be whole.

New appreciation and a tenderness of love shall spring forth from your heart as you see each day more of My plan for thee and thine. Blessings abundant and secure are yours. It is a time of building, stone upon stone, the building of a structure of love and peace that cannot be toppled. My armies surround you, to protect you and shield you from harm, to buffer you against the enemy. Your heart shall sing as you see the marvels I have in store for you. Keep your heart strong and alert, and believe.

Your path is secure. The ravages of time shall not alter your course. Many shall behold My faithfulness to you. Let each day pass as ordained, and they shall bring forth fruit, precious fruit, unto Me. Worry not. Fret not. Tarry not in unbelief, but set your sail to go forward, spurred on by My gentle breezes.

Today is the first day of the rest of your life. Use it wisely. Keep your counsel with Me. Open your heart to receive of My grace and wisdom. Receive as you have given, with joy and delight. Go forth with new hope and expectancy in your heart. I shall not fail thee or thine. You have been through the "Valley of Achor." The Valley of Misery has truly been transformed into the Valley of Hope. Progress, true progress, has been made and shall continue forever. Rejoice and be glad, for out of the ash heap has sprung forth a rose of great value. Its quiet beauty shall be a blessing to many.

Stand firm. Stand tall and straight. Refuse to be jostled. Rely on Me at every turn. Love is all around you. You are not forsaken. Look and see. Thou art blessed, My child.

Rise and shine, for thy light has come. Shine forth for the promises which shall come forth in your lifetime. Shine forth, for the love that is shed forth upon you shines forth from you. Shine forth for My truth shall reign. Shine forth, for the light of the Word comes forth in you and in those you love.

Give out justice, and justice will be returned to you. Love, and you will be loved. Break forth in singing, and those around you will sing. Praise Me, and those around you will praise Me. Give forth of My love, and My love will return to you. What you give forth boomerangs back. Be a joy giver and a peace maker.

In My Father's house are many mansions. I am building one for you. Each room shall be perfect and complete. Each phase must be accomplished in every detail. So, rejoice for the outcome. Let your heart sing in anticipation of the accomplished result.

Raise your voice in song this day. Raise the glorious flag of triumph and praise. Rejoice and sing, for the light, My light, shines in the dark places and brings forth the radiance of a new day, complete with grace and truth, healing and blessings abundant. Let your heart sing. Return your heart to the joy that I have given you. Fear not the present nor the future, for your days are in My hands, and My Spirit goes with you, to bring you peace and love and abundant success. Face each new day with a song in your heart, and trust that I will bring you through unscathed, with nothing missing. Ours is the victory. Rejoice, for the day is at hand!

Keep your feet in the stirrups. Keep moving along the trail. Let each morning find you moving forward in My light. Sing along the trail. It makes the trip easier and more pleasant. Praise along the way. It keeps your spirit right. And finally, keep your focus ever on Me. Forward, ever onward, My child.

The stirrups don't fit well, but keep your feet in them. All will go well with and for you, and you shall see results abundant. Sit lightly in the saddle, and let Me carry you to your destination. Enjoy the sights along the way, and don't become dismayed nor discouraged. The trail is narrow but straight. Just take it day-by-day. As you enjoy the trail and those around you, the journey will become more pleasant. Receive your sight, perception, discernment, understanding and awareness. Let your eyes see and your ears hear the sounds and sights of My Kingdom around you springing to birth.

Blessed is the one whose heart pants after Me in anticipation and desire to know Me better. Their spirits shall be like well-watered plants thriving in the sunshine. Blessed art thou, My child. Let thy blessings flow out to those around you through the laying on of hands and the laying on of prayer. Your requests shall be made known and acted upon. Many shall the blessings be, and many shall bless My name because of thy faithfulness. Minister and give forth in the spirit of love and forgiveness. Press on into My Kingdom, giving forth My blessings. Amen and Amen!

Chapter 21

Promise Fulfilled

*"Now unto Him that is able to do exceeding abundantly
above all that we ask or think, according to the power that worketh in us,
Unto Him be glory in the church by Christ Jesus throughout all ages,
world without end. Amen."*
Ephesians 3:20-21

Restoration it shall be ten-fold. Listen, My dear one. Listen intently and know beyond the shadow of a doubt that all shall be well, that all is in readiness and shall come forth as the radiance of the sun comes forth at dawn. Each promise shall be fulfilled. Every piece shall fit snugly into place as you stand in faith and watch Me work. With vicissitude and strength have I made My way known to you, and shall it not come forth to My Glory, to the Glory of My Name? Let not up your intense faith in My promises to thee and thine.

Reach out! Reach out to that one in need and say, "My Lord will provide for thee. He shall not forsake thee nor abandon thee in thy hour of need," for My angels shall watch over that one in need and bring him through to the other side. Many are the trials of this life, but My love transcends all trials. Let them know of My love for them. Let them know.

Nothing is impossible to Me. Limit not My blessings to you. Steadfastness is all I ask from My children. The fulcrum of My love is trust and steadfastness. There are points of interest along the way, but let your heart rest in the fulcrum of My love for you, contented and free, for I bring contentment, fulfillment completeness and freedom to My blessed children.

Manifest My love in such a way as to overshadow the gathering gloom. Light and bright shall My love emanate from you, as to shine through the gathering clouds and make them as if they were not there. Mountains shall become mole hills in the light of My love for you. I fashion for you an oasis in the desert, a refreshing from My hand to bring you assurance and tranquility. Rest assured, My child, all shall be well, for all is fashioned by My hand for you and unto you. The shoe shall fit like a glove. The shoe of My making shall fit you with ease. The Master Builder has fashioned for you an oasis in the desert, resplendent and complete. Be refreshed. Be at ease, and be at rest in My love.

Set your course by My standards. Do not be afraid to move against the tide. That is when the greatest growth appears. Set your course by My beacon light, and follow on to victory.

Polish your armor. Make ready. Many are the blessings I have in store. Regain your strength of purpose. Know My sustaining power in your life once more. Lighten your load by My strength. Maintain a quiet, peaceful spirit that hears My every word. You shall be ready, and all shall be well. Harken to My words to you, words of life-giving measure. Foreordained are My plans for you. Worship Me in spirit and in truth, for the light of My righteousness shines upon you to bring you to victory.

It shall be as I have said. Hold on to your dream. Be patient, and hold steady. Set your mind on things on high, and let Me work out the things below!

Be removed and lifted up. Be removed from the everyday rigors of life, for I have made for you a stream in the desert, a place of refreshing and rejuvenation, to bring forth new life in many others through your coming apart to be with Me and being refreshed. The plans that I have for you shall be revealed, step-by-step, and you shall know of My benevolence and untold blessings toward you. The axle shall revolve with rapidity as you see My plan for you unfold. Sit upon the horse of My choosing, straight and tall in the saddle, proud to do My will, choosing to forsake other paths, and willing to follow My way for you. Refreshing is My way for you, and resounding with every kind of prosperity and success. Go to it, My child.

Weigh carefully all that I have told you. Let the words of My mouth and the meditations of your heart be one. Keep your eyes open. Be aware of My guiding hand. You shall see, day-by-day, My guidance for you. Open up your heart to receive with thanksgiving and joy. Minister My love as you traverse the way. Rejoice My child. Bask in the warmth of My love for you.

Finish the course I have set before you with joy, not consternation. Begin to use the time allotted to you to the greatest usefulness. You shall know that of which I speak. Tighten your belt. Take in the slack and proceed with diligence and progression.

Forewarned is forearmed. Stand straight and tall with your back to the wind and your shoulders thrown back with determination to finish the course with distinction. Let your steadfastness and determination be known to all. Do not let up your stance of faith, faith in My Word to you, for My Word is like a rock to you that cannot be moved nor swayed. Steady on, My child. The best is yet to come.

Stability is yours from your Father, above. Times of warmth and plenty are on the horizon, soon to be seen and felt and known. Times of plenty, preceded by times of testing and trials, bring forth fruit. The soul knows and perceives and appreciates when the difference is experienced by contrast. Let the fruit of your labor come forth as the rising sun over the mountains. The sun is mightier than the mountains and overcomes the mountains by its light. So shall the mountains of your life be overcome by My light. The light dawns. The new day dawns, filled with splendor and joy. Let My light shine through you, that it might overcome the mountains in others' lives, too, as My light shines through to them, overshadowing the mountains and making them into molehills.

Settle in and be known for your persistent waiting for My Word to come forth, for come forth it shall. Be not weary in waiting, for My Glory shall shine forth as the morning sun shines its rays for all to see. Steady on, My child, with heart poised and waiting for My call to come forth. Rejoice, My child, for unto you shall I give the keys to the understanding of My ways and My call unto thee and thine.

Rest on My laurels, for I have given to you that which you need to give forth of My Spirit. So rest in Me and give forth of My Spirit to the tired and weary of heart. My Spirit shall sooth and comfort and bring joy and peace. So, simply give forth!

A joy too great for words shall come upon you and bring you peace like none you have ever known. Starting tomorrow, you shall be aware of promises I have made to you and of their fulfillment to you. Let your heart take you where it will, for you shall see and be seen in ways you have not perceived before. Let My Spirit flow, and flow it shall with resounding power and love. Strength of will, of My will for you, shall shine through like a beacon light of hope. Stand tall in My Spirit and in My love for you, and let all see the magnitude of My love for them through My love for you, and see they shall.

Did I not say and did it not come forth? Rejoice, rejoice, I say, for the heavens ring forth with joy for the magnitude of My Grace and Glory as was shown. Treasure these moments, and rejoice, as you see the future drawn ever into the present. Glimmers of My blessings for you have you seen and revelled in. Now go forth with My promises resounding in you heart, for the fulfillment is sure and the foundation has been laid with soundness. Be refreshed and renewed in the clarity and surety of My steadfast grace and provisions for you. The ship of My provisions for you has set sail and shall find safe and sure harbor. It is My will for you to come forth unemcumbered by the burdens of the past, to step proudly into the future, bearing My banner of peace, secure in My love.

Get a straight arrow-bead on the future, and with singleness of mind, head in that direction. Zero-hour is at hand, with no time now for vacillating or variations. Keep your focus on Me at the end of your sights. Struggle is not necessary for success; indeed, it is a hindrance. Set your will, give your will to Me and be at peace, confident that We shall prevail.

Wave from afar as you traverse this road, intent upon the fulfillment of My Word to you. Wave from afar to the demands upon your time that try to steal away your time with Me. Wave from afar to the negative advice from well-meaning doubters. Wave from afar to their like-minded cousins, defeat and dismay, for unto you I give the gifts of straightforward trust, faith and understanding. Portents of doubt and gloom cannot touch you. Blessings and fulfillment are your portion.

Register the peace of your Father. It is yours today. Peace comes and peace goes, but this is an everlasting peace that fills your days and your nights with song and praise. Show forth this peace in your day-to-day comings and goings, for it shall shine forth as a beacon light to show forth the work of your Father.

Rest this night in My love for you, My child. Rest and continue to rejoice as you see My plans for you unfold with rapidity and joyous anticipation. You are blessed beyond measure. Rest, My child, rest.

Keep a steady gait, steady and sure. Continue on with steadfastness and faith. Onward and upward. Faint not, but keep your eyes on Me. Rest assured. My strength shall sustain you in all things. Let not down your stance of strength and faith. Your life's goal looms mightily and safe from harm in My hand, ready for My bidding to come forth, and come forth it shall at the appropriate time and place. So rise up in your spirit, ready to maintain and retain all that I have given you to know and walk in. Your future is sure. All is set forth in My Book of Life as I have pre-ordained, and it shall come to pass as I have said. You are blessed. Rejoice and be glad.

It is time. The time is here to know that for which you have been painstakingly prepared. Buckle on your breastplate of peace, brought forth through My Word to you. Within My will for you is found that which shall delight your heart and cause you to rise up and bless My Name. Watch for it. Watch for the fulfillment of your dream to bring forth, to bring to birth. Many times you have looked forward to see the fulfillment of your dream. Now, you shall see it in the now. Receive unto your heart the fulfillment of the promise. Watch with anticipation, for unto you have I given the desires of your heart. It has been proclaimed! So shall it come forth!

You have asked in faith believing. You shall receive. Buckle in, for the journey is long, but it won't be hard, for you have Me carrying the load to lighten your way to bring you success. Be sure of your source and proceed with diligence. Be of a stout heart. Press in with an unfaltering spirit. Lead the way with pride in Me, and others shall follow with lighthearted joy.

Chapter 22

The Field Is Ripe For The Harvest

*"Then saith He unto His disciples, The harvest truly is plenteous,
but the labourers are few; pray ye therefore the Lord of the harvest,
that He will send forth labourers into His harvest."*
Matthew 9:37-38

Simple are the ways of My followers. Simple, straightforward ways. Be not bogged down with detail in the coming days. Let My Spirit lead you in simplicity and truth. Reversed shall be the financial burden, reversed to bring forth blessed peace. Brightness, cheeriness and radiance shall mark the formation and duration of My work for you. Direct your energies with simplistic design. My ways for you are laid out to bless thee and thine. Rejoice and be glad, My little one. The field is ripe for harvest.

Study to show yourself approved, a workman that need not be ashamed. Fill up your heart with My Word. It shall be a lamp unto your feet and bring peace along the way. Many shall know of My Word to you, and of the miracles that Word has wrought, and of the miracles that Word shall continue to bring to pass. Let My Word bring forth in you true joy, undisturbed by circumstances or seasons. Show forth My Word to you through the blessed assurance I have given you. Astounding shall be the results.

Circumcision of heart is taking place, a cutting away of the old. Behold, all things are new. Continue to magnify My Name through obedience to My Word. I am with you, My child, to help you to persevere. Proceed, proceed, proceed, to carry forth with joy and perseverance all that I have laid before you. Great shall be your elation. Glory in the Highest!

Stay with it, My child. Stick with it, for the rewards are sure. Perseverance pays off ten-fold, with blessings and rewards in abundance. Unto the strong and devoted go the victory and rewards. Maintain a steadfastness unto the end. Stretch forth your arms to receive in victory My accolades to you. Radiate My goodness to you. Let it be a treasure to be seen and felt and known. Blessed is the one who comes in the Name of the Lord!

The time of suffering is drawing to a close, and in its place will be refreshing. Bend your ear to Me, and hear My direction to you. Train your thoughts to maintain their direction. Teach your heart not to wander. The times are set to bring to you refreshing and rejuvenation. Be not concerned, for they shall come, and you shall know your direction. Steady on, My child. Walk with a firm gait and conviction in your heart. Be strong. Feed upon My Word. You need nourishment. Be strengthened. Move out slowly, but surely. Breakneck speed is not My Way. Be not as the race horse that breaks loose with blinding speed only to be disqualified in the end. Step-by-step, step out as I lead.

It shall be clear to you, the path that you shall take, and the way will be bathed in light so that you shall not miss it nor be distracted nor sidetracked. The vision is strong and shall remain strong unto its fulfillment. Worry not nor be distraught, but know that what I have planned for you shall be, and you shall rejoice and be glad. Carry on with a song in your heart and determination to finish the way with honor. My blessings go with you, My child. The refreshing of mind, body, soul and spirit shall come and buoy you up. Press onward! Press onward!

The way is mapped. Go with ease. Steady as you go. Maintain a steady, even gait. Cruise!

Your help cometh in the Name of the Lord. Lean not upon others for assurance. Be assured. Bountifully have I dealt with you. Hold fast to that which you have been given: My peace, the joy of your salvation, the hope of your calling and the promise of that yet to come. Blessed art thou, My child, from everlasting to everlasting. Begin to ascertain with enlightenment, for you shall begin to see flesh and meat form upon the foundation of that which has been laid. So be it!

Strap on your riding gear, and continue on My way. The way is rigorous, but My way is sure and trustworthy. Mere words of compassion and strength shall guide you along and buoy you up for the journey. Refer back often. My dealings with you have been sound and sure. Stand back often and survey the panoramic picture. It will keep you standing on solid ground. Painstakingly have I lead you to bring you into right standing and into position for the illumination of the promises and miracles to come forth. So, be at peace, My child. Let each day be a symbol of My grace to you. Let each day be evidence of My love for you, and let each day bring forth the fruit and joy that comes from that love and grace. Streams of living water shall again flow from you to bring forth good fruit in season, and we shall rejoice together. Struggle not with unseen provisions. Remain alert and prepared to receive.

Quiet yourself before Me. Let your heart be at peace. Many times have I brought you from the security of My lap into the vast unknown, but I have been with you and protected you, and you have learned and grown and prospered.

Listen, and you shall hear. Retain your sense of expectancy. Delight yourself in Me, and let that delight shine forth from you. Let your face shine with Sonshine. The Spark of Life has been rekindled and reigns within.

Stretch forth your wings and fly. Be not bound by outward appearances. The joy of the Lord is your strength and your song, and the buoyancy for your wings. Take off and soar!

Eye hath not seen nor ear heard the wondrous works the Lord brings forth for those who love Him. Restrict not your thinking as to what you can see. Let your thinking scan the far vistas of My creative power. Master the art of maintaining open ended plans, that My plans might always become, and remain, paramount in your life. Closed-ended plans stagnate and cease to function. My plans for you are as the butterfly, free and unrestricted to your views of them. Stymie not, and seek not to mold them into your own conformity of sight. Let loose of your plans, and let Me take hold of the helm once again. Blessed is the one who sees, yet does not dictate the outcome, but leaves that to Me. Follow with dexterity and delight, with a loose grip on the future. Let Me lead in all things. Let Me bring forth creatively and freely.

The "Year of Promise" comes forth, riding on the wings of My provision. Blessed is the one who knows of My promises to him and moves forth in the assurance of those promises. The transition time has truly begun. With it has come My peace, joy and reflections of My dealings with you. Continue to reflect back on, and ponder, My past blessings to thee and thine. You will find therein a vast storehouse of blessings. You have prayed in faith, believing. Now, watch it come forth, and come forth it shall. The measure of faith that I have given you once more stretches forth and expands to bring forth blessings.

Keep a straight and steadfast course. Keep your eyes on the goal. Be prepared to stretch forth your wings as never before in ways that will be astounding to you. The pace shall alter in style, but not in intensity.

Blessed assurance is yours that the victory is complete. The final countdown has begun, and the road is paved with the precious jewels of My constant and abiding love towards you. Relentless and constant has been your desire to please Me, and constant and relentless shall be My hand to you in your behalf. The thorn has been rent from your side, never again to return to plague you. You shall respect yourself, and you shall be respected. Go forth now with assurance and boldness, to walk tall in My Spirit, bearing My Banner of truth and righteousness over thee and thine. Rejoice, My child! The time has come forth for rejoicing. Sing and rejoice, for I have done all things well. Hallelujah!

Today marks the beginning of the blazing forth of new trails. You shall be among this new breed of trailblazers. But a trailblazer must be disciplined. Fulfill your destiny. Accept your mantle of obedience. Let go of your own desires and inner cravings. Be Holy, as I am Holy. Rejoice, as I shall rejoice at your freedom.

Steady yourself for the onslaught. Time shall become precious, and blessings shall abound beyond measure. The time of quiet reflection is drawing to a close, and in its place, following on its heels, will be a time for action as led by Me. Stretch out your wings to meet the new day. You shall be pleased.

Stand still, and know that I am God. Be ready and eager, but moved only by Me. Little-by-little, every obstacle shall be removed, every piece put neatly in place. Place your hand in Mine, and step-by-step, we shall see the vision come into focus and into fulfillment. You are blessed, My child, to see and know the joy of step-by-step fulfillment, brought forth by Me, with loving attention to each and every detail.

Tarry not along the way. There is much to be done. My Spirit shall lead you in all that you shall do, and you shall know delight and satisfaction. Many shall come to know of My leading and guiding power through the relating of My guidance to you. Proceed with delight, delight in My Word, delight in My guidance for you, and delight in the guidance of your loved ones. It is a new day, filled with bright anticipation and joy.

Now, bloom where you have been planted. Brighten the lives of others by My Spirit within you. Heighten their awareness of Me through your relationship to Me. Many I shall send you to warm and direct toward Me. The stream of humanity shall be endless, but My Spirit shall guide you in every instance. Let not go of My hand. Fasten your gaze on Me, and move forward as I shall lead. Glorious shall the journey be, and delighted shall you be, and those around you. Lift up your head and your heart, and rejoice in the new day, filled with its joys and treasures from Me.

Set your heart to hear My Word continually to you. Be a transmitter of that Word, a magnifier of My Word. Be at peace in all that you shall do unto Me, for I am your guidance and your strength. Never forget from whence cometh your guidance and you strength. It comes from Me! Lay aside all hindrances of the body, soul and spirit, and fly with Me with freedom and exhilaration.

Stand straight and tall in My Spirit. Let your heart be strong in the knowledge of My love for you. You cried out, and I answered. You shall continue to prosper and to grow in the light of My Spirit, in the light of My love for you. Behold! All things are new! The old has passed away, and behold, the new has sprung forth as the noon day sun. Rejoice, My child, and be glad. Many have longed to see this day come forth in their lives. Your day has come. Give forth of My love to you. Give forth with a gentle, loving and understanding heart, filled with the blessings of My love to you. Break forth into singing, My little one. Break forth into the new day with song. Shalom! Amen!